THE
RAMNUGGUR BOYS

His Majesty King William IV, Royal Patron of the Regiment, 30 July 1830, by Sir David Wilkie
(The Royal Collection © 2002, Her Majesty Queen Elizabeth II)

THE
RAMNUGGUR BOYS

14th/20th King's Hussars 1715–1992

Foreword by H.R.H. The Princess Royal

JOHN PHARO-TOMLIN

Museum of
The King's Royal Hussars
in Lancashire
(14th/20th King's Hussars)

To all who have served in the 14th/20th King's Hussars, and to their Families

Published privately by
the Museum of The King's Royal Hussars in
Lancashire (14th/20th King's Hussars), Fulwood
Barracks, Preston, Lancashire PR2 8AA

British Library Cataloguing-in-Publication Data
A catalogue record for this book is available from
the British Library.
ISBN 0-9542772-0-1

CARTOGRAPHY BY WILLIAM EDGE
Designed and produced by
DAG Publications Ltd, London
Designed by David Gibbons
Edited by Michael Boxall

While every effort has been made to trace copyright
holders and seek permission to use illustrative
material, the publisher wishes to apologise for any
inadvertent errors or omissions and would be glad
to rectify these in future editions.

Italics have been used to highlight the *14th/20th
King's Hussars* and its predecessors, *The Royal
Hussars* and its predecessors, and *The King's
Royal Hussars*. Battle honours and the principal
battles have been similarly emphasised. All the
material in this book is in the public domain, and
no classified information has been included. Any
opinions expressed are those of the author, and
do not necessarily reflect official policy.

Printed and bound in China by
Compass Press Ltd

CHRONOLOGY OF REGIMENTAL NOMENCLATURE

1715	*Dormer's Dragoons (14th)* raised
1776	Designated *14th Light Dragoons*
1798	Designated *The 14th (or Duchess of York's Own) Regiment of Light Dragoons*
1830	Designated *The 14th, or The King's, Regiment of Light Dragoons*
1861	Designated *14th (King's) Hussars*

1759	*20th Inniskilling Light Dragoons* raised
1763	Disbanded
1779	*20th Light Dragoons* resurrected
1783	Disbanded
1791	*20th Jamaica Light Dragoons* raised
1802	Designated *20th Light Dragoons*
1818	Disbanded
1861	*20th Light Dragoons* resurrected
1862	Redesignated *20th Hussars*

1922
amalgamated as *14th/20th Hussars*

1936
became *14th/20th King's Hussars*

1992
amalgamated with
The Royal Hussars (Prince of Wales's Own) to become
The King's Royal Hussars

CONTENTS

Her Royal Highness,
The Princess Royal,
Colonel-in-Chief 14th/20th
King's Hussars, 1 July 1969
(Catherine Moubray)

BUCKINGHAM PALACE

For the twenty-three years that I was Colonel-in-Chief of the 14th/20th King's Hussars the Regiment has occupied a special place in my life. From my first visit at the age of nineteen until the parade in 1992 when it joined The Royal Hussars to form The King's Royal Hussars, I have got to know hundreds of its members and their families; I have become very aware of its history and I have followed with delight its many achievements.

As this book shows, the Regiment has always been a close knit, family organisation with tremendous pride during both peace and war. The battle of Ramnuggur, from which the title is taken, was marked by the outstanding commitment of all ranks. The most recent example of this has been the exceptional conduct of the Regiment during the Gulf War.

I am very pleased that the history of the Regiment and its forebears is now recorded in this book, which, together with 'The Tenth' and 'The Cherrypickers', will form the background history to my new Regiment, The King's Royal Hussars.

Anne

ACKNOWLEDGEMENTS

This list names all those former members of the *14th/20th King's Hussars* and friends of the Regiment whose contributions, in advance, have enabled this book to be published. Names of contributors have been shown as accurately as possible. Ranks have been omitted; decorations and titles where known are given. Any omissions are unintentional.

D. A. Adesile
K. Alcock
F. Alvin
S. T. Arrowsmith
A. F. B. Ashbrooke
C. P. A. Astley Birtwistle
J. F. T. Baines
C. J. Balfour
Mrs Jean Ball (formerly Justin)
C. W. N. Bankes
J. J. D. Barrow
M. J. Bartley
R. D. Baxter, JP, DL
G. R. D. Beart, MBE
D. L. de Beaujeu, OBE
W. H. Bentley, MBE
S. G. E. Bland
C. J. T. Blease
D. J. Bowes-Lyon
W. G. C. Bowles, OBE
A. J. Bradshaw, OBE
S. M. Brady
A. H. I. Bridges
H. M. Brodie
L. P. J. S. Bromley
W. H. Brown
S. P. Bryant
M. Burgess
R. G. Burgham
D. L. Burt
A. W. Byrde
G. A. Camburn
N. St. C. Cameron
J. C. Cameron-Hayes
P. B. Cavendish, CB, OBE, DL
R. S. C. Cavendish
S. Chappell
C. V. Clarke
Sir Peter Clarke, KCVO, JP
P. R. H. Clifford, TD, MFH
J. R. Clifton-Bligh
J. Close
S. Codrington
V. L. Colborne
T. A. Colquhoun
N. B. Corbould
J. C. Cornish

R. F. Cornish, CMG, LVO
B. S. Crossland
M. A. Cullinan
The late A. E. Cundy
J. D. Cunningham
Miss Laura Currás Lino
K. Davies
T. A. Davies
M. G. S. Davis
C. R. K. Dean, OBE
J. C. V. Denning
Dennis Murphy Campbell
Mrs Rosemary Dickson
H. M. Dixon
M. P. Dodworth
K. S. Dowding
B. J. M. Draper, MBE
J. Dromgoole
M. H. G. Drury
M. P. Dunn
W. R. T. Edge
P. N. Eliott-Lockhart
Mrs Anne English
J. J. Escott
A. J. C. Evans
J. V. Eyre, JP, DL
S. J. Farling
R. J. L. Fellowes
P. T. Fenwick, OBE
D. J. Ferguson
R. F. Fernsby
A. H. Fincham
R. Finlay
G. S. Fletcher
D. J. Flowers
M. O. J. Fooks
A. P. H. Fradgley
S. R. M. Frazer
J. A. Frost
Mrs Sally Gandon
F. T. Gant
P. D. W. Garbutt
S. C. Garner
C. P. Garnett
E. T. Gimlette
G. Giuseppi
Mrs Angela Goodhart
A. A. Gossage
J. H. Graham

J. H. Grainger
The Hon. Jeremy Grey
A. T. Grieve
Mrs Anthea Groves
B. R. Hamilton
I. J. Hardbattle
P. B. Harding
A. C. Harman
P. Harman
Mrs Diana Harris
R. Harrison
C. Hazell
J. W. Hedges
J. A. Henderson
R. G. Hews
E. J. N. Hicks
T. P. Hicks
D. J. Hill
E. D. Hill
M. N. Hill
P. A. Hoare
K. M. Hodson
T. D. Holderness Roddam
M. R. Holland
R. Y. Holland
E. E. Hooper
J. F. A. Hope
M. L. A. Hope
Jerwood Foundation
C. F. Johnston
J. M. Kelly
Dr Christine Keown
S. E. Lang
Dr. D. G. H. Maggs
C. J. Mann, MFH
R. J. Mann
J. M. Marcelle
J. Mawer
N. J. McDermott
I. McDonald
J. C. W. MacGregor
J. R. Metherell
M. K. Milne
N. J. Milverton
G. J. Mitchell
E. J. Morris
Mrs Sheila Mossé
P. J. Nutsford
A. Ogden

Mrs Frances Oliver
J. N. N. Orr
Mrs Evelyn Osborne
R. J. Owen
J. D. F. Palmer
J. R. M. Palmer
Sir Michael Palmer, KCVO
C. A. Park
C. E. Paul, MC
C. A. Pemberton
Miss Alice Pharo-Tomlin
E. J. Pharo-Tomlin
J. A. Pharo-Tomlin
N. H. Phillips
J. Podesta
N. G. T. Polley
Miss Kathleen Potts
C. K. Price, CBE
J. P. Rawlins
B. W. D. Rensburg
Mrs P. Richardson
A. C. G. Ross
C. C. G. Ross
D. Ross
E. T. Ross
I. R. Rumble, BEM
R. G. Russell
R. Sakalauskas
The Salters' Company
R. Sands
A. Sanford
D. E. R. Scarr, CBE
T. P. Scott
G. L . Scott-Dickins
G. P. Shakespeare
E. Sheen, MBE
A. A. Shipton
A. R. D. Shirreff, CBE
K. F. Shurety
J. F. Sibley
I. Simpson
A. R. E. Singer, OBE
J. R. Smales
I. Smith
M. A. Smith
D. R. Staniford
L. V. Stell
B. G. Stocker

W. J. Stockton, OBE
D. R. Stoddart
P. L. B. Stoddart
A. Stuart-Mills
S. W. G. Suchanek
N. G. Sudall
G. L. Sullivan, MBE, MC
Mrs I. Sutherland
C. Sym
Dr J. N. Symons, TD
G. A. L. C. Talbot
T. C. Tayler
C. M. I. Tennent
Mrs Betty Thompson
G. H. R. Tilney, MBE
R. A. U. Todd
P. M. Tonks
R. F. Tyson
The late M. A. Urban-Smith, MC
J. A. Valdes-Scott
T. Vale, MBE
D. A. J. Vaughan
M. J. H. Vickery
P. R. G. Vickery
T. F. Villiers-Smith
M. W. E. Wade, MBE
J. G. Wainright
E. G. W. T. Walsh
J. R. E. Walters
P. C. R. Wates
W. R. Whitwell
H. A. O. Wicks
D. S. Wild, BEM
D. A. J. Williams, MBE, JP
L. G. D. Williams
M. A. Williams
N. Williams
T. G. Williams, CBE
C. D. C. Willy
R. P. Winch
Sir Nicholas Winterton, MP
R. N. Winterton
A. R. B. Woodd
D. J. B. Woodd
P. J. Workman
W. Zbierajewski

PREFACE

It has been an honour to be invited to write this history by the Chairman of the Regimental Association, Lieutenant-Colonel Peter Harman and his 'book committee' consisting of Major-General Peter Cavendish, Lieutenant-Colonel Christopher Ross and Colonel David Woodd; all have made important suggestions on what to cover, given me full editorial freedom and looked at the finished script. In recording the Regiment's 277-year life, I have tried to concentrate on what was important, interesting or amusing. The material contained has been my decision, as have any omissions. Every effort has been made to put in a wide variety of pictures and focus on those which have not appeared in previous histories. Former members of the Regiment have kindly sent in many photographs, but unfortunately it has been impossible to include hem all.

I am indebted to Major-General Sir Michael Palmer, the last Colonel of the Regiment, for his support and to Captain 'JC' Cornish, the Regimental Secretary (North) and to Mrs Christine Swift. Former members of the *14th/20th King's Hussars*, their relations and friends have helped generously with sponsorship and their names are on the page opposite. My thanks are also due to the late Lieutenant-Colonel Peter Upton for his invaluable advice on producing this book, as the result of his experience writing *The Cherrypickers* and *The Tenth*. Edmund Southworth, the Lancashire County Museums Officer, has given support to this project throughout, and Dr Stephen Bull, the Military History Curator, has read and advised me on the text as it was written; as an established author, his help has been indispensable. An enormous amount information and pictures have been provided by Douglas 'Tiny' Hill, who joined the Regiment in 1936, is the author of *Nobody's Own*, the History of the *20th Hussars*, and has been our regimental historian for the last twenty years. My thanks must go as well to the author and journalist, Andrew Lycett, and to the military historian Charles Messenger.

The Photographic Archive Department at the Imperial War Museum have provided many of the Gulf War pictures, and the help of Ms Jenny Spencer-Smith, Dr Alastair Massie and their staffs at the National Army Museum, has been invaluable, as has been the guidance of David Fletcher at the Tank Museum, Bovington. I am also grateful to Mrs Sian Cooksey at the Royal Collection for facilitating the loan of pictures of our two Royal Patrons.

Copies of family pictures and papers have been generously provided by Charles Cottrell-Dormer, Sir John Hervey Bathurst, Bt., and Mrs Terence Gossage, the granddaughter of Brigadier-General Edmund O'Brien. Russell Burgham, 2nd Troop Leader 'C' Squadron at Medicina, has provided a useful personal account of the battle. In an illustrated history, clear photographs are essential, and I am indebted to the two commanding officers of *The King's Royal Hussars*, Lieutenant-Colonel Jonathan Powe and Lieutenant-Colonel Tim Allen, for making pictures and silver available for inclusion, and I also much appreciate the assistance of officers, senior ranks and soldiers in *The King's Royal Hussars* during my many visits to Tidworth. The photography carried out by Steve Day of Salisbury, at Aliwal Barracks, and by Craig Smith of

Norwyn Photographics, at Preston, has been of exceptional quality. My thanks also go to Major William Edge for his excellent maps which have so enhanced this book.

Sean Hawkins of the Ancient House Bookshop in Reigate has given much advice on marketing and distribution. I also wish to thank David Gibbons, Tony Evans and Meredith MacArdle, of DAG Publications Ltd, for their imaginative design of this book and for being so congenial to work with; their contribution to this project has been decisive.

Finally, I also could not have written this book without the encouragement, guidance and constructive criticism from my three children, Sally, Edward and Alice, and my fiancée Christine; the support all four have given me has been indispensable.

John Pharo-Tomlin
Leigh, Surrey,
May 2002

1 INTRODUCTION

This history is a snapshot of the *14th/20th King's Hussars*, starting with the foundation of the Regiment in 1715, as *Dormer's Dragoons*, and the forming of the *20th Inniskilling Dragoons* in 1759. It covers both regiments until the amalgamation of 1922, and ends with the further amalgamation with *The Royal Hussars* in 1992, to form *The King's Royal Hussars*. The historical period is that from the First Jacobite Rebellion until the Gulf War.

The *14th* fought its first battle at Preston, shortly after being raised, and in the second half of the eighteenth century, spent nearly 50 years in Ireland. The *20th* had to wait 30 years to go into action, but then fought very aggressively in America, Africa and Europe; being a junior regiment, it suffered four disbandments, whenever the size of the Army was cut. *The Battle of Ramnuggur*, during the Second Sikh War, was one of the more important engagements of the *14th Light Dragoons*; in this battle, the Commanding Officer, Lieutenant-Colonel William Havelock, lost his life with 44 others killed or wounded, hence the title of this book.

Right: Colonel Sir Felton Bathurst Hervey, Bt. in the uniform of ADC to the Duke of Wellington, which appointment he was given after the Battle of Waterloo (Courtesy Sir John Hervey-Bathurst, Bt.)

Throughout its existence, the *14th/20th King's Hussars*, and its forebears, have had the good luck to be involved in many of the unusual campaigns during the nineteenth and twentieth centuries. Both regiments saw action in America, and in the Peninsular War, where the *20th* were the only cavalry at the Battle of Vimiero; the *14th*, under Colonel Felton Bathurst Hervey were awarded more battle honours than any other cavalry regiment. The Regiment's first Victoria Cross was won by Lieutenant James Leith during the Indian Mutiny, and a second was won in the Boer War, by Major Edward Brown, later Browne-Synge-Hutchinson.

In the First World War the *14th* and the *20th* served with distinction in Europe and the Middle East, and both had commanding officers killed, Colonel George Cook of the *20th* and Colonel 'Pongo' Hewitt of the *14th*. Likewise Regimental Sergeant-Majors Goddard of the *14th* and Rabjohn of the *20th* both won the Military Cross. In 1920, against

Far left: Colonel Edward Browne-Synge-Hutchinson, VC, who was awarded the Victoria Cross for conspicuous bravery during the Boer War

Near left: Lieutenant-Colonel George Cook, CMG, DSO, who was killed commanding the 20th Hussars on 26 March 1918

Below: Regimental-Sergeant-Major J. Goddard, OBE, MC. After retirement he was elected Mayor of Weymouth from 1938 to 1945 (Steve Day; courtesy The King's Royal Hussars)

Turkish nationalists, the *20th Hussars* carried out the last charge in history of a complete regiment of British cavalry against well-armed troops. During the Second World War the*14th/20th* saw action in Persia and Italy, but missed the campaigns in North Africa and North West Europe. Post-war the Regiment spent much of its time in the British Army of the Rhine (BAOR), the cockpit of the Cold War, in between operational tours in Cyprus and Northern Ireland, where it took as many casualties as any Royal Armoured Corps regiment. The climax of the history of the *14th/20th King's Hussars* was reached when the Regiment served with the International Coalition Forces at the liberation of Kuwait in 1991.

Like all organisations, businesses and political parties, the Regiment has had its ups and downs, and I have made no attempt to 'skate over' the latter. The *14th Dragoons* did not serve with credit at the Battle of Prestonpans in 1745 and their premature withdrawal during the Battle of Chillianwalla brought some disgrace to the *14th Light Dragoons* for many years, and even led to tragedy. The comparatively minor role assigned to the Regiment during the Second World War was a serious disappointment to all ranks, and rankles to this day.

The *14th/20th King's Hussars* have proved to be unrivalled as a close-knit family regiment. Sons have followed fathers and

Right: The Hollands – Farrier Sergeant-Major P. Holland, Sergeant R. Holland, Staff Sergeant R. Holland, Sergeant P. Holland and WO2 M. Holland

sometimes grandfathers throughout its history. In the Peninsular War, Private Charles Cureton joined Captain Brotherton's troop in the *14th Light Dragoons*, became the Cavalry Commander, as a brigadier, in the Second Sikh War, but was killed while attempting to restrain Lieutenant-Colonel William Havelock at *Ramnuggur*; his son joined the *14th* as a Cornet, but he too was to be killed, at *Chillianwalla*. Farrier Sergeant-Major Percy Holland served in the *14th* and the *20th Hussars* between 1887 and 1908, and his son Sergeant Robert Holland was also in both regiments from 1912 to 1921; his three grandsons, Robin, Peter and Michael, all joined the *14th/20th* between 1957 and 1961, becoming members of the Sergeants' Mess in the course of time. Major Harold Tilney joined the *14th* as a subaltern in the Boer War; his son 'Freckles' commanded the *14th/20th* at the Battle of *Medicina*; his grandson Godfrey was Second-in-Command during the Gulf War, and his great-grandson, Angus, has just joined *The King's Royal Hussars*.

During its near 300-years' history, there has been a strong tradition in the *14th/20th King's Hussars* of mutual respect and friendship between all ranks, of putting a high price on achieving professionalism and also in finding every opportunity for enjoyment. This book strives to tell this story.

2 DORMER'S DRAGOONS

When Queen Anne died in 1714, the strongest claimant to the Crown was James Stuart, known to his supporters as James III, but to his enemies as 'The Old Pretender'. The 1701 Act of Settlement, however, prevented his succession to the throne because he was a Catholic, so it passed to George, son of Sophia, Electress of Hanover, who became King George I of England.

The King was not over enthusiastic about coming to England, preferring life on the flat North German Plain, between the rivers Aller and Weser; an area the *14th/20th* would get to know well many years later, but which they would find less appealing than had George. The new king's main interests in life were said to be food, horses and women, with which sentiments the Regiment would have rather more sympathy. Given his lack of zeal towards his new realm, the mood in the country

Below: Lieutenant-General James Dormer, founder of the Regiment, 22 July 1715, by Van Loo (Mark Mason; courtesy Charles Cottrell-Dormer)

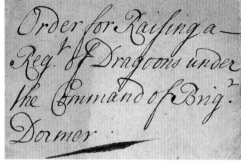

became ill-disposed towards him, and many felt that James Stuart should be on the throne. He, however, was in France at this time, waiting to lead an invasion and planning a number of uprisings during the year. So the decision was taken to increase the size of the army, and the *14th Dragoons*, among others, were raised in July 1715 by Brigadier-General James Dormer, of Rousham Park in Oxfordshire, whose house stands to this day. He was ordered to form up his regiment, also known as *Dormer's Dragoons*, in Shrewsbury. Many of the soldiers came from Ireland and had previous army service, which was to bode well for the first battle fought four months later.

Although still in France, James was proclaimed 'King James III', by the Earl of Mar on 6 September 1715. Eighteen Scottish lords joined Mar's army of over 5,000 men, and the First Jacobite Rebellion began. The uprising started successfully, and Perth was captured, but Mar then sent 1,500 troops south to occupy Preston, whose conquest was to be short-lived.

On 11 November, Major-General Wills was ordered to advance on Preston via Wigan, to prevent the insurgents reaching Manchester. Wills' forces comprised Pitt's Horse, four regiments of dragoons, including *Honeywood's (11th)*, and *Dormer's (14th)*, with three regiments of foot. They left Wigan early on 12 November and arrived south of the river Ribble later in the day. The town was heavily defended and the road leading to Lancaster was barricaded.

Dormer's Dragoons dismounted and attacked vigorously but were driven back. Wills therefore set fire to houses around Lancaster Avenue, from where snipers were shooting. After receiving reinforcements, a cease-fire was negotiated, and the Jacobites surrendered. The Regiment lost three men and sixteen horses; Dormer was wounded, the first of many colonels to become casualties in battle during the Regiment's history, and three soldiers were also injured. The first battle by the *14th*, therefore, ended successfully and made its mark in defeating the First Jacobite Rebellion. It is an interesting coincidence that this engagement took place so near to where the Regiment was to establish its Home Headquarters and Museum in the twentieth century.

Left: Authority, signed by King George I, for General Dormer to found the 14th Dragoons (Mark Mason; courtesy Charles Cottrell-Dormer)

Below: Transcription of the Authority

George R

Whereas we have thought fit that a Regt of Dragoons be forthwith Raised under your command for our service which is to consist of six Troops of One Serjeant, Two Corporals, one Drummer, One Hautbois, and Thirty private Dragoons, including the Widows men in each Troop. These are to authorize you to by beat of Drumm or otherwise to raise so many Volunteers as shall wanting to compleat to said Regimt to the above numbers, And when you shall have list fifteen men fit for service of the said Troops, You are to give notice to two of our Justices of the Peace of the Town or County wherein the same are, who are hereby Authorized & Required to view the said men and certify the day of their so doing from which day the said fifteen men and any Commissioned and non Commissioned officers of such Troops are to Enter into our Pay and you are to cause the said Volunteers to be Raisd & Levyed as aforesaid to march under the command of such Commissioned Officers as you shall Direct to Shrewsbury in Shropshire the Place xxxxxxxxxxx Appointed for the Rendezvous of the said Regt; And all Magistrates, Justices of the Peace, Constables and other our Officers whom it may concern are hereby Required to be assisting unto you in providing Quarters, Impressing Carriages and otherwiseas these Shall occasion. Given at Our Court of St James's this 23rd day of July 1715. In the first year of our Reign.

To our Trusty & Wellbeloved James Dormer Esq.
Brig Genl of Our forces, & Col of one of Our   By his Majtys Command
Regts of Dragoons or to the Officer or Officers
appointed by him to Raise Volunteers for that Regt.   Wm Pulteney

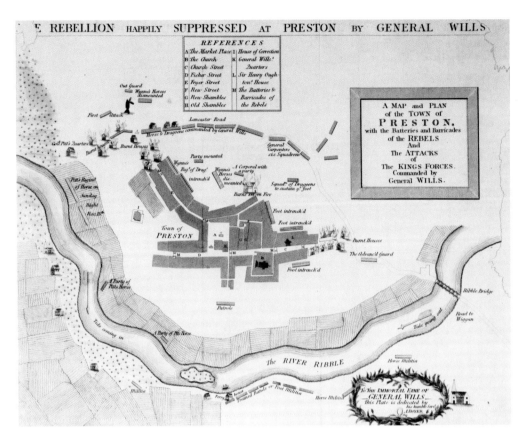

Left: Map of the Battle of Preston (Courtesy Harris Museum Preston)

Below:
The Jacobite surrender at Preston, watched by Dormer's Dragoons (Courtesy Harris Museum Preston)

Right: *A dragoon of 1742*

Many prisoners were taken and initially were herded into Preston Parish Church. Later, a batch of 1,500 was escorted to Lancaster Gaol where *Dormer's Dragoons* stayed for the next six months, so beginning their ties with Lancashire. In May 1716, the *14th* moved to Lincolnshire and, a year later, to Ireland where they were to remain for twenty-five years. In Ireland, troops were quartered in different stations throughout the north and south, moving from time to time. In 1720 Lieutenant-General Clement Neville succeeded Dormer as Colonel. After a distinguished career in other fields, General Dormer died in 1741 and was buried in the family tomb at Long Crendon in Buckinghamshire.

In 1727 King George II acceded to the throne, and while at first no more popular than his father, led a European army to victory against France at Dettingen in 1743, the last British sovereign to lead an army in battle. This action gave him necessary authority and ensured the eventual defeat of the Young Pretender. In 1737, Lieutenant-General Archibald Hamilton became Colonel, and the *14th* was also known as *Hamil-*

ton's Dragoons. Hamilton did not command the Regiment in battle, which was fortunate for his reputation, because the *14th*'s contribution to the defeat of Prince Charlie was to be less auspicious than its contribution to the defeat of the Prince's father in 1715.

In 1745, Charles Edward Stuart began the Second Jacobite Rebellion. Despite a chequered start, this charismatic young man, known as 'The Young Pretender', had raised an army of 1,500 men. The *14th*, back from Ireland, were ordered to move to Leith as the rebels advanced on Edinburgh. The Regiment then joined Colonel Gardiner, who was commanding the 13th Dragoons, at Corstorphine to the west of the city. As the Highlanders advanced, the inexperienced dragoons in both regiments were withdrawn to join the town guard at Coltbridge, where they dismounted. The 13th and *14th* were then forced into a hasty retreat as the rebels made a further and unexpected advance. Both regiments' horses bolted, a manoeuvre described by some critics as the 'Canter of Coltbridge'.

On 20 September, Lieutenant-General Sir John Cope gathered his army, including the 13th and *14th Dragoons*, and began to advance up the coast towards Edinburgh to take up what he had thought to be a strong position at Prestonpans. But the Prince, who was leading his forces in person, surprised Cope at first light on the 21st. Both regiments were still mounted, but unable to charge, so the battle ended in a rout. This caused much amusement to the Jacobites at the time and to armchair critics later. However, unlike the situation at Preston in 1715, the soldiers were inexperienced and were kept mounted when they should have been on foot and vice versa. Colonel Gardiner was killed; many officers and soldiers in both regiments fought bravely, notably Major Bowles of the *14th* who, despite having his horse killed under him, continued to fight dismounted and received eleven wounds.

On 13 January 1746, *Hamilton's Dragoons* were moved to Falkirk and took part in the ensuing battle, alongside the *10th* and *11th Dragoons*, under the command of Lieutenant-General Hawley. Although Cope had superior numbers, his army was without artillery and appears to have been surprised at dinner when the rebels made their first attack. The initial cavalry charge was successful, but a counter-attack by the Highlanders drove the Dragoons back and they withdrew in some disorder. After the battle, the *14th* were left behind to patrol the approaches to Edinburgh.

Following Prestonpans and Falkirk, neither the 13th nor the *14th* were asked to take part in the battle of Culloden. While this was frustrating at the time, it may have been lucky for both regiments not to have been present at an engagement which was to acquire a reputation for atrocities. In 1747 *Hamilton's Dragoons* returned to Ireland, and twelve years later the *20th Dragoons* were raised at Enniskillen.

3 NOBODY'S OWN

In 1756, Great Britain and Prussia began the Seven Years War against France and, much of the army having been sent overseas, chiefly to Flanders and to Canada, more troops were needed for home defence and coastal protection, and in Ireland for Internal Security duties. Six new regiments of light dragoons were therefore raised, and one of these was the *20th*, founded at Enniskillen in the north of Ireland in 1759.

The Regiment was known as the *20th Inniskilling Light Dragoons* (not to be confused with the 6th Inniskilling Dragoons, which became the 5th Royal Inniskilling Dragoon Guards). The establishment was twelve officers and 232 men, in four troops. The Regiment was commanded by Lieutenant-Colonel Sir James Caldwell, Bt, of Caldwell Castle, on Lough Erne in County Fermanagh. As the numbering of regiments started formally in 1746, the *20th* did not take the name of their colonel; during the nineteenth century they were known colloquially as *'Nobody's Own'*, being the only cavalry regiment without a patron. Despite this label, the *20th* were to enjoy many successful campaigns, though in lean years, they would be disbanded four times.

While the *14th* went into battle immediately after it had been raised, the *20th* had to wait for more than thirty years before seeing action. Its service in Ireland was fairly routine, its main employment apparently being the arrest of disorderly elements in the course of its internal security duties. When the Seven Years War ended in 1763,

and the threat from invasion diminished, the *20th* was disbanded for the first time. In the Hon J. W. Fortescue's *History of the British Army*, the *20th* merited no more than a mere mention.

In 1775 the War of American Independence began, and light, mobile troops were seen to be needed. The *14th Dragoons*, who were still in Ireland, became the *14th Light Dragoons*; the conversion took two years because all arms, saddlery and equipment had to be changed. Minimum height for recruits was lowered, and the height of troop horses was reduced to 15 hands. A regiment of *light dragoons* was therefore cheaper to equip and maintain.

The *20th Light Dragoons* were resurrected on 27 March 1779 at Bury St Edmunds from troops of other cavalry regiments, including the *11th Dragoons*. Commanded by Colonel R. Burton Phillipson, they moved to Colchester and, during the summer, to Plymouth. They spent much of this period in pursuit of smugglers along the south coast, an established role for dragoons at the time. Although these duties must have been fun, they did not make the soldiers popular because local inhabitants usually benefited from the smugglers' activities. But patrols were also needed to watch for the landing of enemy agents.

At this time, most cavalry regiments were frequently on the move, unlike the infantry which was already beginning to establish county links. Thus in 1780, the *20th* found themselves in Canterbury, Margate, Broadstairs and the surrounding villages. This was after an outbreak of 'ague' (malaria) in the ranks, where it was considered that the healthy air of the Isle of Thanet would allow effective convalescence.

In March 1781 the *20th Light Dragoons* moved to Lenham Heath near Ashford to assist in maintaining law and order, and in October, to Macclesfield and then Manchester, their first visit to the County. The following year they were back in East Anglia, around Bury St Edmunds once more. After the unfruitful four-year siege of Gibraltar by France and Spain, the Treaty of Versailles was signed in 1783, ending the war. Despite the continuing threat to British interests, the government saw fit to reduce the army again, and the *20th Light Dragoons* were disbanded once more.

The French Revolution began in 1789, and a year later, the Declaration of the Rights of Man in the National Assembly led to unrest in the West Indies by the indigenous population, particularly in Jamaica. The government agreed to reinforce Jamaica with two infantry battalions and a cavalry regiment, and in 1791 the *20th* was raised for the third time, by Lieutenant-Colonel H. Farrington Gardiner, as the *20th Jamaica Light Dragoons*, and an interesting period of 28 years in the Regiment's life was to follow. The establishment was 300 deployed in four troops. At first recruitment was difficult; the West Indies had a justly appalling reputation for disease, from which one commanding officer was to fall a victim. Lack of home leave also deterred potential recruits, so the shortfall had to be overcome by transfers from other regiments.

Left: 14th Light Dragoon, 1776 (before conversion)

Right: A 20th Jamaica Light Dragoon 1794, wearing the Regiment's unique 'tin' helmet with hair mane and alligator below badge

Among those transferred was one Lieutenant Rollo Gillespie from the Carabineers, an officer with a chequered past; the first officer to transfer from that regiment to have problems, but not the last. As a Cornet, he had fought a duel in Ireland and killed his opponent. At his subsequent trial for murder, the jury, which included several half-pay officers, brought in a verdict of justifiable homicide, and in due course, he was given the King's Pardon. He was later to distinguish himself in action in San Domingo where he was severely wounded.

In the summer of 1792, the *20th* sailed and arrived at Spanish Town in November, under strength with only 150 all ranks, which was further reduced within six months by which time the commanding officer and 32 soldiers had died of yellow fever. The costs of maintaining the Regiment were reluctantly met by the Jamaican Assembly, and at first the colonial government was hardly getting value for money. But a year later this was to change when unrest by the freed slaves, known as *Maroons*, started. The rebellion was intensifying around Montego Bay, some fifty miles from Spanish Town, and only approachable through difficult country.

On 12 August, Colonel Sandford, who was now in command, set off with a detachment of 130 men from both the 18th and *20th Light Dragoons*. Unfortunately, it was ambushed in the close country, and the colonel, with fourteen of his soldiers, was killed. As the terrain favoured the guerrillas, the cavalry bore the brunt of the losses incurred during the following period of rough skirmishing, but the Maroons were eventually surrounded and forced to surrender.

At the same time, another rebellion was breaking out in San Domingo (now the Dominican Republic). While this was a French colony, the settlers were no longer loyal to the recently declared French Republic and sought help from the Governor of Jamaica. An expedition landed in San Domingo in September 1793 with reinforcements from many quarters. These were in due course to include part of the *14th Light Dragoons* who left Waterford in Ireland without their horses.

While these rebellions were starting in the West Indies, in June 1794, two troops of the *14th* left County Tipperary for Ostend where they were attached to the 8th Light Dragoons with orders to defend the port against the French revolutionaries. The force included the 33rd of Foot commanded by Colonel Arthur Wellesley, later to become the Duke of Wellington. In this generally unsuccessful campaign the *14th* saw a good deal of service. The army, under the command of the Duke of York, was forced back to the river Meuse, and at the battle of Boxtel on 14 September was defeated by the French with the loss of about 1,500 men, mostly Germans, but including two from the *14th*. On 30 December, in freezing weather, which allowed the cavalry to cross the iced-up rivers, the Allies succeeded in driving the French back over the river Waal. In January 1795 the *14th* fought in further actions at Geldermalsen, inflicting heavy casualties on the enemy without loss. At Buren and at Elst, on the river Lech, the Allies were less successful. While the *14th* still appear not to have incurred any losses, superior enemy forces caused the Allies to withdraw into Westphalia and on to Bremen. After this,

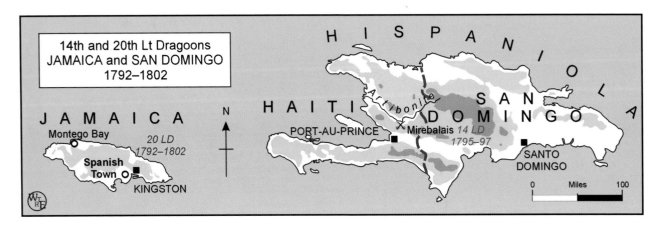

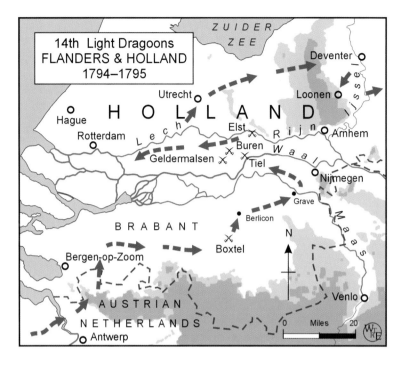

the two troops of the *14th Light Dragoons* were incorporated into the 8th Light Dragoons, ending the regimental involvement in this European campaign.

The main body of the *14th* landed in San Domingo in July 1795 and were mounted on horses brought over from America. For the next two years, they were engaged in operations against the well-trained rebels, claiming to be loyal to France. The country in San Domingo and Haiti was generally unsuitable for cavalry, and yellow fever was rife, causing many deaths. The *14th*, 18th and 21st Light Dragoons, however, fought a most successful action at Le Mirebalais on the border of Haiti and San Domingo.

On 2 June 1797, a detachment, commanded by Lieutenant-Colonel Arthur Carter of the *14th*, drove a force of some 1,200 rebels from a commanding position into the river Artibonite, capturing the fort intact including six guns and a large quantity of ammunition. While there were no battle casualties, the climate took a heavy toll, and when the Regiment returned to Chelmsford in October 1797, it was at skeleton strength.

At this time, the *20th* were still in Spanish Town and were brought up to strength with reinforcements from those regiments sent home from San Domingo. On 25 December 1799, as a consequence of his excellent service with the Regiment and previous successful attachment in San Domingo, Rollo Gillespie was appointed to

Right: 20th Jamaica Light Dragoons Regimental medals (one of which appears to have been misengraved), presented by Lieutenant-Colonel Rollo Gillespie (Courtesy The King's Royal Hussars)

command the *20th*. As the military need for the Regiment to remain in Jamaica was diminishing, the House of Assembly reported their unqualified satisfaction with the performance of the *20th Jamaica Light Dragoons* but asked that they be returned to England because of their cost to the Island. Lieutenant-Colonel Gillespie was awarded the sum of one hundred guineas, 'to be by him expended in the purchase of a sword, as a testimony of the high esteem in which his conduct is held by this House'.

The Regiment departed on 28 June 1802, disembarked at Southampton and marched to barracks in Guildford. The next few months were spent on recruiting and attending to a disciplinary inquiry into the conduct of the Colonel. One of the officers, Major Cameron, had instigated a formal complaint that Gillespie had fraudulently submitted muster rolls in Jamaica and had received allowances to which he was not entitled, i.e., drawing pay for dead men. This was in fact an established practice, which allowed the extra money to be spent for the benefit of the Regiment. Happily Lieutenant-Colonel Gillespie was honourably acquitted of the charges on the grounds that he had done this for the good of the service and with the sanction of the Commander of the Island. Major Cameron was less fortunate, being informed that His Majesty had 'no further occasion for his services', a judgement with which few would argue. But one must wonder what had caused such disloyalty by an officer to his colonel. They must have had a serious row at some time with Cameron coming off the worse.

Shortly afterwards, Gillespie transferred to the 19th Light Dragoons, with whom he served with great distinction in India and Sumatra. Ten years after leaving the *20th* he was killed in action in Nepal, so ending a brave but seldom dull life, in the service of his country.

Above: *Sergeant, 20th Light Dragoons, 1808*

Below: *South Coast Patrol by 20th Light Dragoons, by W. B. Wollen* (Hugo Burnand; courtesy Peter Fenwick)

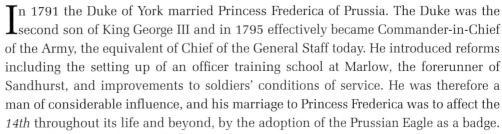

4 PRINCESS FREDERICA

In 1791 the Duke of York married Princess Frederica of Prussia. The Duke was the second son of King George III and in 1795 effectively became Commander-in-Chief of the Army, the equivalent of Chief of the General Staff today. He introduced reforms including the setting up of an officer training school at Marlow, the forerunner of Sandhurst, and improvements to soldiers' conditions of service. He was therefore a man of considerable influence, and his marriage to Princess Frederica was to affect the *14th* throughout its life and beyond, by the adoption of the Prussian Eagle as a badge.

While stationed at Chelmsford, the Regiment was sent to Harwich to greet and escort the Duchess of York on her arrival in England. To mark the occasion, on 26 July 1798 the King approved the adoption of the title *14th* (or *Duchess of York's Own*) *Regiment of Light Dragoons*, and Princess Frederica became the 'Royal Patroness'. The uniform facings were changed to orange, which was the livery colour of the Royal House of Brandenburg. The Regiment kept its new title until 1830, when King

Below: Introduction of the Duchess of York to the Royal Family in 1793 (Steve Day; courtesy The King's Royal Hussars)

William IV became Royal Patron. According to Cecil Woodham-Smith, 'The Princess was an eccentric lady, who disliked going to bed, and when she did, remained there for only an hour or two, preferring to live surrounded by at least forty dogs, monkeys and parrots.'* Not surprisingly, the Duke of York was consistently unfaithful to his wife over many years, and the childless marriage ended in separation. She spent the rest of her life surrounded by her animals in Weybridge, where she died on 6 August 1820.

In 1799 the *14th* were based at Canterbury; they would remain in the south for the next eight years. In 1800 their establishment was raised to 900, consisting of ten troops of 90 men; four new Guidons (the equivalent of infantry Colours) were also received. At around the same time, according to anecdote, the regimental band was due to perform at an important engagement in Dover, but was unable to do so having drunk far too much alcohol the night before. The band of the Royal Sussex Regiment had to replace it at short notice. As a consequence 'Royal Sussex' became the Quick March of the *14th* and *14th/20th*, and later 'Sussex by the Sea' was played as the Regiment marched off parade.

*Woodham Smith, Cecil. *Queen Victoria: Her Life and Times*

The *20th* had also been stationed in the south, and in March 1805 came a welcome break in the monotony of home service when 300 dismounted men of the Right Wing, under Lieutenant-Colonel Charles Taylor, were embarked for service in the Mediterranean. En route for Gibraltar, the convoy passed Nelson's fleet lying off Cape St Vincent with HMS *Victory* in the centre.

In May 1805 the Left Wing, under Lieutenant-Colonel Sir Robert Wilson, embarked at Portsmouth without horses, in a force commanded by General Sir David Baird, bound for the Cape of Good Hope, then a Dutch possession, which posed a threat to the East India Company's merchantmen.

Reports of a French fleet bound for the West Indies brought a change of orders and the convoy altered course for Salvador in Brazil to procure horses, arriving on 10 November. It then sailed back to the Cape, arriving off Table Bay on 4 January 1806. At Cape Town, the *20th* found that the Dutch settlers had already, frustratingly, surrendered. Cape Colony was taken under British rule, and the Left Wing was first ordered home, and then instructed to return to South America, again.

An expedition against the Spanish colonies in Latin America reached the River Plate in October 1806 and landed at Maldonado to the east of Montevideo at the end of the month. The *20th* fought dismounted alongside the 38th of Foot and the 21st Light Dragoons with gunfire support from the ships. Although the Argentinians were soundly routed, reorganisation was precarious. Fortunately the *20th* managed to get sufficient horses and spent the time foraging for the garrison and the fleet.

On 13 January 1807 the expeditionary forces re-embarked at Maldonado and landed near Montevideo three days later. Four cavalry regiments were involved: the Left Wing of the *20th*, and elements of the 9th, 17th and 21st Light Dragoons, with naval gunfire support. After landing the force came under heavy artillery fire, but thanks to the gallant leadership of the commander, Sir Samuel Auchmuty, whose horse had a leg shot off under him, the operation was successful, and the *20th* captured three guns. The Spaniards fled into the city, which was stormed on 3 February. In September the remnants of the Left Wing were ordered home and on arrival were sent to Guildford to recruit.

Turning back two years. In June 1805 the Right Wing of the *20th* sailed from Gibraltar to Malta to procure horses. While they were there, Nelson defeated the French at the Battle of Trafalgar on 21 October, which cost him his life. This historic victory lifted the threat of invasion to the United Kingdom, but Napoleon still denied the ports he controlled to British trade.

In late October the Right Wing of the *20th* re-embarked and landed at the Bay of Naples on 20 November. In January 1806

Left: Princess Frederica, by P. E. Stroehling (The Royal Collection © 2002, Her Majesty Queen Elizabeth II)

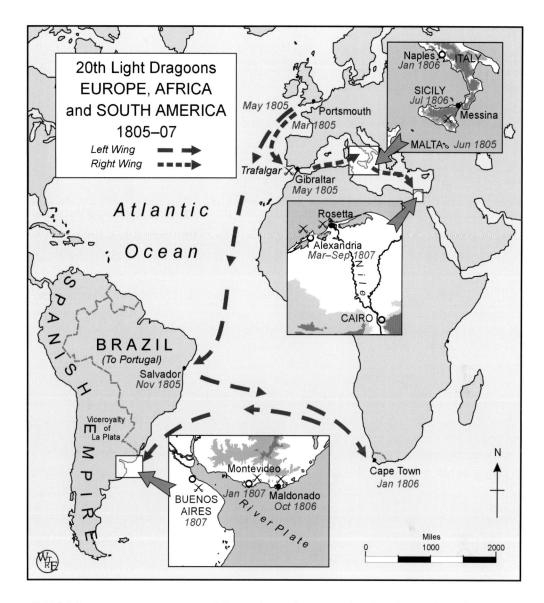

Left: Lieutenant-Colonel Sir Robert Wilson

all British troops were evacuated from the Italian mainland and transferred to Sicily because of the threat from the southward advance of some 30,000 French forces. Despite the superior numbers of the enemy, the British commander, General Stuart, decided to launch an attack across the straits because the French were widely scattered. The British forces, including a small detachment of the *20th*, crossed on 26 June. The French commander was taken by surprise and, despite concentrating a large force at San Pietro di Mada, was defeated on 4 July. This successful engagement would have been more decisive had there been sufficient transports available to take a greater number of cavalry.

On 7 March 1807, one squadron from the Right Wing of the *20th* sailed from Messina as part of an expedition commanded by Major-General Fraser Mackenzie, bound for Alexandria which was held by the Turks and friendly to Napoleon. The *20th* landed in rough seas accompanied by one thousand infantrymen. Despite a spirited resistance, the city surrendered, but Fraser decided that his position was precarious and exploited to Rosetta and Ramanieh, some forty miles away.

After the successful occupation of Rosetta, a large Albanian force counter-attacked and forced a withdrawal, but a further attack against the village of El Hamid, four miles to the south of Rosetta, was easily checked by the *20th*'s squadron. Turkish reinforcements with their own cavalry arrived, and a fierce battle ensued, the men of the *20th* being surrounded. One man was lost, six horses were killed, and the Squadron Leader, Captain Delaney, was taken prisoner. A galloper, Private Tremble, was sent to get help and fought his way through the Turkish cavalry, to bring two infantry companies to the support of the squadron. Private Tremble's name is remembered for posterity and, had official awards been given for gallantry in those days, he would have received such a decoration.

Following this difficult operation, the British force made a fighting withdrawal to Alexandria, losing some eight hundred officers and men killed or captured. The troops remained in Egypt until September 1807 while negotiations were conducted with the Turks, which included the repatriation of all British prisoners.

At the end of 1807, the *14th Light Dragoons* were dispersed throughout the South of England, routinely employed and parading at ceremonial functions. A part of the *20th Light Dragoons* was based in Maidstone and another part was still in Sicily. Both regiments were awaiting the call to Sir Arthur Wellesley's army in Portugal for the beginning of the Peninsular War.

Left: *Officers of the 14th Light Dragoons, 1808*

5 THE PENINSULAR WAR

In 1807 Great Britain was standing alone in opposition to Napoleon, and her Royal Navy was heavily deployed in a rigorous blockade of the European coastline. Anxious to bring Portugal under the 'umbrella' of the so-called Continental System (the embargo on British trade), that country being the sole remaining open market available to the British, Napoleon decided to invade Portugal via Spain, which would serve the dual purpose of blocking the gap and perhaps enabling him to take control of the Iberian Peninsula.

In November 1807, by permission of the Spanish, General Junot brought an army into Portugal and seized Lisbon; the Portuguese royal family fled to their colony in Brazil. In May 1808 Murat brought an invasion force of 100,000 men into Spain, Charles IV and his son Ferdinand were forced to renounce the throne, and Napoleon's brother Joseph was crowned King of Spain.

A Spanish mission to London appealed for military assistance and Major-General Sir Arthur Wellesley was sent with temporary command of an expeditionary force of 11,000 men to eject the French from the Peninsula. The troops, including the *20th Light Dragoons* under Lieutenant-Colonel Charles Taylor, sailed from Cork on 13 July 1808 and landed at Mondego Bay, a hundred miles north of Lisbon on 1 August.

The *20th* led the advance on the capital, supported by the 60th Rifles and the Rifle Brigade. While the Regiment was on the Torres Vedras road, Junot launched a major attack against Vimiero Hill. In the evening of 20 August, Sergeant Landsheit of the *20th* rode in from the outpost line and told General Fane that the French were approaching from Torres Vedras. Fane complimented him for his alertness and told him to report direct to Wellesley at midnight. The *20th* were out of sight but not out of

Above: Lieutenant-Colonel Charles Taylor, killed at Vimiero (Steve Day; courtesy The King's Royal Hussars)

Right: The Battle of Vimiero – the 20th Light Dragoons are visible at the bottom right corner (National Army Museum)

earshot of the battle, and Colonel Taylor was determined to influence matters. After many requests, the *20th* were allowed to charge, which they did, galloping through the French lines and putting the enemy to rout. Unfortunately, during the violent battle, the Colonel was shot through the heart by a sniper. Like many cavalry actions the battle ended in some confusion, but the French were put to full retreat. The *20th* lost twenty men killed and thirty horses.

Opinions as to the Regiment's performance at Vimiero differ; according to Lady Longford's biography of Wellington: 'The *20th Light Dragoons* dashed forward at a breakneck gallop which ended in fiasco, the horses bolting, most of their riders casualties, the colonel dead and little damage inflicted on the enemy. This was the first but far from the last time that Wellesley saw British cavalry go out of control.' *

Nevertheless, eleven regiments were commended by Wellesley, including the *20th* who were awarded their first battle honour: *VIMIERO*. Regrettably, Wellesley's superior Generals Dalrymple and Burrard arrived to take over. These two old idiots

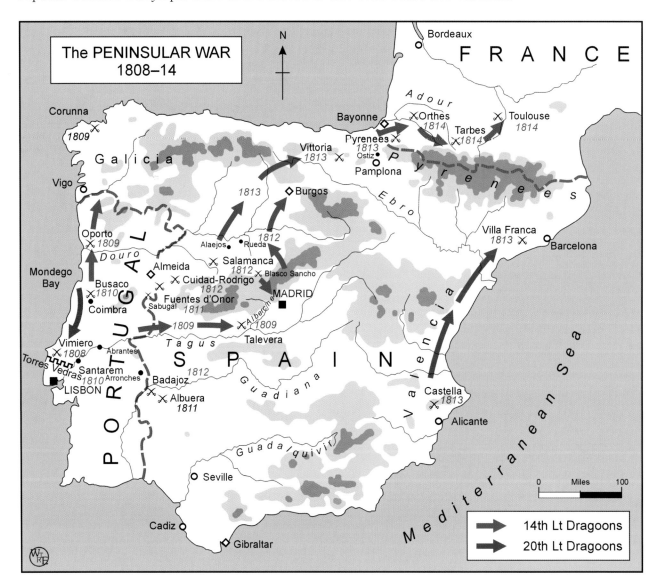

*Longford, Lady Elizabeth. *Wellington: The Years of the Sword*

Above: Colonel, later General, Samuel Hawker. (Steve Day; courtesy The King's Royal Hussars)

negotiated and signed the Convention of Cintra which allowed the French to evacuate all their forces from Portugal in British ships. This caused a tremendous outcry in England, and as Wellesley was the third signatory he was recalled with them to a court of inquiry at which he was the only one exonerated.

After Vimiero, the *20th* marched to Lisbon and were joined by the *14th*, who arrived on 23 December. In the north-west, Lieutenant-General Sir John Moore was conducting a series of withdrawals which ended at Corunna. A total of 24,000 men were successfully evacuated, but in 1809, Moore, a potential rival to Wellington, was killed.

As resistance to France in Italy was gathering strength, a force of about 13,000 men, including 300 from the *20th Light Dragoons*, embarked for Sicily. On 11 June 1809 they sailed from Milazzo to Ischia in the Bay of Naples, the passage taking thirteen days because of unfavourable winds. The garrisons of Ischia and its neighbouring island Procida were disarmed and taken prisoner. In October, a troop of the *20th* sailed with an expedition to capture the islands of Zante and Cephalonia off the coast of Greece. This troop remained there while the Regiment concentrated at Messina for three years to assist in the defence of Sicily. In September 1810 the French attempted to invade at Punta del Faro. However, Privates Jacob Longman and John Green gave early warning of the attempted incursion by galloping through the enemy, brandishing their sabres, and thereby raised the alarm. 1,000 prisoners were taken by the defending forces and both *20th* soldiers were awarded medals for their bravery.

In April 1809, Wellesley returned to command the British army in Portugal. The *14th Light Dragoons*, under Colonel Samuel Hawker, formed the advance-guard on the march to Coimbra. In May, they were brigaded with the 16th and *20th Light Dragoons* under Major-General Cotton, and were reviewed by Wellesley, whose first objective was to expel the French from Oporto. Two squadrons of the *14th* under Lieutenant-Colonel Neil Talbot were attached to a Portuguese force, commanded by the British Marshal William Beresford, whose task was to intercept the French should they retreat to the east. The remaining three squadrons, under Colonel Hawker, advanced to Oporto on 10 May. The army reached the Douro where two squadrons of the *14th* were detached and crossed upstream at Barca-de-Avintas. Meanwhile a fierce engagement was taking place nearer the city, so the *14th* and the German Brigade advanced down the right bank, which prompted the French to retreat.

The leading squadron of the *14th*, under Major Felton Bathurst Hervey, charged and routed the enemy's rear-guard. On the French side, General Laborde was unhorsed, General Foy was wounded and 300 prisoners were taken. The *14th* had to fight their way back and several men were killed or wounded, including Hervey who lost his right arm. On 12 May 1809, Wellesley issued a general order congratulating the *14th Light Dragoons*, but the Regiment had to wait until 1837 to receive *DOURO* as a battle honour, which was conspicuously absent from the Guidon in 1832.

Above: Lieutenant-Colonel Felton Bathurst Hervey (Courtesy Sir John Hervey-Bathurst, Bt.)

Wellesley's success at Oporto cleared Portugal of the French, who had incurred 4,000 casualties; British losses amounted to 23 killed and 98 wounded; the victory perhaps went some way to avenging the death of Sir John Moore at Corunna. In June, after the *14th* had pursued the worn-out French troops through the mountains, the army concentrated around Abrantes. The subsequent advance into Spain caused the enemy to retreat, but the French counter-attacked the Allied troops formed up at Talavera. General Mackenzie deployed an infantry division and a cavalry brigade in a forward position in a wood on the right of the river Alberche, and they were attacked on 27 July. The *14th* were therefore ordered across the river to cover the infantry and skirmish until nightfall, during which time, two men were wounded and nine horses were killed. The *14th* returned to their defensive positions and supported the infantry during heavy fighting the next day.

Later, the French launched a strong attack against Major-General Sherbrooke's division, only to be repulsed. The *14th* and 16th Light Dragoons and the 49th Regiment were brought forward, and the Foot Guards advanced again. This simple-sounding manoeuvre was in fact perilous and the Allied army was in danger of annihilation. However, the courage and determination of the Allies prevailed and the French retreated. The *14th* had three men and 21 horses killed, Colonel Hawker was wounded, as were four other officers and six men. Hawker was later awarded a gold medal, and in 1820 the Regiment was awarded *TALAVERA* as a battle honour. Substantial French reinforcements forced Wellesley to withdraw into Portugal, the *14th* moving back to Santarem in December. Soon afterwards Wellington was rewarded with the title of Viscount.

On 14 March 1810, the Regiment advanced to Arronches, on the frontier, and in June moved north to Almeida. It was attached to the Light Division, taking outpost duty with the 16th Light Dragoons and the 1st Hussars of the King's German Legion. While the opportunity to relieve Ciudad-Rodrigo did not arise, the *14th* supported the 95th (Rifle Brigade) in laying ambushes. Early on 11 July, bodies of French infantry and cavalry were seen so the Brigadier deployed the cavalry through a defile, after which they rode up a hill alongside and fearlessly charged the French infantry square. The enemy held their ground and fired so effectively that the commanding officer, Lieutenant-Colonel Neil Talbot, and eight men were killed with 23 men wounded. Despite the French withdrawal, the opportunity to pursue was not taken.

After Talbot's death, Lieutenant-Colonel Felton Bathurst Hervey took over command. Hervey came from a family known even today for unconventional behaviour. His father, a grandson of the 3rd Marquis of Bristol, was understood to have got into serious debt which he could not manage so, in 1785, he bought a pair of pistols at a gunsmith's in Piccadilly, paid for them, loaded them and shot himself through both temples, while still in the shop. Despite this parental misfortune and the loss of his right arm, Hervey's leadership of the *14th* was to prove outstanding throughout the campaign.

In July, after the fall of Ciudad-Rodrigo, the Regiment withdrew to Almeida, where it faced a large concentration of the French Army. An active night of patrolling was followed by fighting at daybreak. One sergeant was killed; one officer, one soldier and four horses wounded. After resisting the greater enemy numbers for some time, the British were pulled back, and the *14th* were commended on 'withdrawing in a most soldier-like manner, despite the superior opposition'.

Following Marshal Massena's substantial invasion of Portugal, the British were forced into further withdrawal on 24 September. Captain Thomas Brotherton's squadron of the *14th* was part of the cavalry rearguard which protected the Light Division's four-mile retreat on to more favourable ground. The three squadrons covering the withdrawal held off four French squadrons, which lost thirty men. Next day, the *14th* covered the final part of the Light Division's retreat to its defensive positions at Busaco. Unfortunately, while carrying out a reconnaissance, Captain Percy was captured.

At the battle of Busaco, the *14th* were in reserve but subsequently protected the army's move back to the fortified lines of Torres Vedras. During this fighting withdrawal, the *14th*, 16th, the Royals, German Hussars and Bull's Troop Royal Horse Artillery defeated a very strong force, almost annihilating a French cavalry regiment, but the *14th* took some losses. While the enemy believed victory was assured, the lines of Torres Vedras blocked their further progress and the Regiment put out forward patrols. The French accordingly withdrew during the night of 14/15 November. The *14th* captured a number of enemy stragglers before Marshal Massena could occupy a new position at Santarem. The Allied army was based at Cartaxo, ten miles south of the French positions, the Regiment providing outposts.

Poor conditions and sickness forced Massena to retreat. On 6 March 1811, finding Santarem deserted, Wellington ordered his army forward in pursuit. On the 8th Captain Babington's squadron successfully charged four squadrons of French dragoons at Venta-de-Serra, capturing fourteen men and their horses but losing two men and horses. The Allied armies continued to press the retreating French, taking part in a number of skirmishes and actions including one at Sabugal on 3 April, until the enemy reached Salamanca where they were reinforced and resumed their advance.

Marshal Massena sought to relieve Almeida, which was suffering from the Allied blockade. Having made contact with the enemy, the *14th* withdrew, and on 3 May, Lieutenant John Townsend pulled his pickets back under heavy fire towards Fuentes d'Oñoro on the Spanish side of the frontier. At the same time, Captain Brotherton's squadron was heavily engaged at Pozzo-Vello nearby. The reorganised French army, however, attacked suddenly at Fuentes d'Oñoro, and the fighting became so desperate that Wellington later said that this was the closest he came to defeat in the Peninsula. Nevertheless, stubborn resolve was to prevail, and on 5 May the *14th* and the Royals covered the movement of the army's right flank at Nave d'Aver, ten miles to the south of Fuentes d'Oñoro. One squadron charged a battery of French artillery, but the squadron leader, Captain Robert Knipe, was killed, and Lieutenant John Townsend took over. Bathurst Hervey had his horse killed under him and was badly bruised in the right leg by an 8-pound shot entering his sabretache but which was slowed down by a thick book inside.

The French made a further attack on the positions at the rear of the village, forcing the cavalry outposts to withdraw and cutting off the artillery battery. But it was not well co-ordinated and there were signs of indiscipline in the enemy ranks, so the advance was checked and the situation turned to the Allied advantage. Captain Norman Ramsay, the battery commander, led his mounted gunners in a spirited counter-attack. Captain Thomas Brotherton led his squadron to block the pursuing troops and General Charles Stewart personally captured General Lamotte, the French commander. The *14th* had three soldiers killed, six officers, including the squadron leader Lieutenant Townsend, six sergeants and 21 rank and file wounded. After this fierce encounter, Bathurst Hervey was rewarded with a gold medal, and the Regiment received *FUENTES D'ONOR* as a battle honour.

The French now regained the initiative and Marshal Marmont advanced with a large army towards the border. The Light Division was therefore ordered to move

Below: *Patrol of 14th Light Dragoons in the Peninsula, known as 'The Flag of Truce', by W. B. Wollen (Steve Day; courtesy The King's Royal Hussars)*

south, covered by the Royals and a squadron of the *14th*. Two thousand French cavalry, six thousand infantry and ten guns attacked, but the British counter-attacked and defeated the enemy, with little loss to the Allies. Marmont nevertheless continued his advance to the Estremadura region, causing the British to withdraw from Badajoz. The Allies then moved up to besiege Ciudad-Rodrigo, the *14th* again deployed on outpost duties, and the French advanced in great numbers with a view to breaking the siege.

On 25 September 1811, Marmont launched fourteen squadrons of the Imperial Guards against the Allied army, driving back the outposts at Carpio to the west of the town. The Lancers of Berg followed up but were driven back by squadrons of the *14th* and 16th Light Dragoons, and Carpio was back in Allied hands. A further attack forced the Regiment to withdraw once more from Carpio into a strong defensive position on the border while the French moved back into Spain. During these actions and afterwards, the Regiment had one officer and several soldiers wounded. In fact Bathurst Hervey was fortunate not to have been killed himself; a French officer, when starting to make a cut at him, saw that he could not defend himself, being without a right arm, so checked his cut, brought his sword to the salute and rode on; Bathurst Hervey's gallantry was matched by his luck. Despite its operational successes, the Regiment's strength was reduced by two troops during the winter of 1811–12.

Ciudad-Rodrigo was captured in January 1812, after which the Regiment moved south to take part in the siege of the fortified town of Badajoz. As the French moved on Albuera, the *14th* protected the Allied withdrawal and skirmished with the enemy's advance-guard. During the night of 10/11 April Badajoz was successfully stormed; the siege had cost the Army 4,760 casualties including six generals wounded and four colonels killed. After the town was taken Wellington lost control of his troops who subjected the wretched civilian populace to an atrocious orgy of sack and rapine.

Five days later the Regiment was in action against several regiments of French cavalry, and a party from the *14th*, under Lieutenant Edward Pellew, captured a picket of 22 French dragoons.

On 16 June the Regiment formed the advance-guard on the march towards Salamanca, losing a sergeant and a trumpeter in a skirmish. The enemy retired behind the Douro and the *14th* pursued to Tordesillas. In July Marmont launched his counter-offensive and successfully made several river crossings. Wellington therefore concentrated his army in a withdrawal from Rueda to Alaejos covered by the Regiment. The French sent a cavalry brigade, under Brigadier-General Carier, to press the British left. The *14th Light Dragoons* and 1st German Hussars were ready for the French cavalry, and in the course of some hard fighting, General Carier was taken prisoner. In the ensuing battle, the *14th* and German Hussars, with other support, drove back the French cavalry and charged the broken infantry lines. The Regiment had eighteen men and twenty horses killed, three officers, including Captain Brotherton, 34 men and eighteen horses wounded.

On 22 July, the battle of Salamanca began with the *14th* skirmishing with the enemy's forward troops. The French attempted to gain the road to Ciudad-Rodrigo by turning the Allied right flank, but Wellington quickly ordered his divisions forward and the Regiment supported an attack on the enemy's left. Two *14th* squadrons reinforced Brigadier-General D'Urban's Portuguese brigade, and turned the enemy's flank. The

French army was then driven from the field with heavy losses. The Regiment had several men and horses killed and wounded. Captain Brotherton, though still affected by the wound received on the 18th, again mounted his charger and was again wounded. The *14th Light Dragoons* were awarded *SALAMANCA* as a battle honour, and Bathurst Hervey was presented with another gold medal. Salamanca was considered by some to have been Wellington's most important victory in the Peninsular campaign.

On 26 July, as the pursuit continued, a patrol of *14th Light Dragoons* and 1st German Hussars, led by Corporal William Hanley, captured a 30-strong party of French troops, including a colonel, at *Blasco Sancho*, to the east of Salamanca. In recognition of this action, the patrol was specially commended by the army commander, given a monetary award, and the officers presented Corporal Hanley with a silver medal. As the *14th* and the Germans were short of horses, those captured were shared out between the two regiments.

Elsewhere, Wellington was concerned about Marshal Suchet's army in Valencia and persuaded the Commander-in-Chief in Sicily and Naples, Lord William Bentinck, to send troops to the east coast of Spain. A force of 7,000 men including part of the *20th Light Dragoons* landed unopposed at Alicante on 9 August, and was reinforced by more of the Regiment by the end of the year. Early in 1813, an advance to the north began, and on 3 March the *20th* drove in the French outposts at Alcoy. On 12 April, the Regiment took part in the battle of Castella after which the French retired in disorder. On 13 September, at Villa Franca, the *20th* and the Brunswick Hussars charged a 2,000-strong French force and caused it to withdraw. This was no mean achievement, the Allies being outnumbered three to one, but the Regiment suffered a number of casualties. At the end of 1813, the *20th* was dispersed with four troops on the east coast of Spain, four troops in Sicily and two troops in England, at Maidstone.

In the west of the Peninsula, after Salamanca, the army advanced to Madrid, and the *14th* established its RHQ at Getafe, to the south of the city, where it took up outpost duties. However, after Wellington left the capital to carry out the siege of Burgos, the French sent in reinforcements making a withdrawal necessary. On 16 November 1812, the Regiment drove back a large body of French lancers, but had several men killed and wounded. Bathurst Hervey was again in the thick of things

Above: Delpini –
Captain Milles's
charger, 1811 (Steve
Day; courtesy The
King's Royal
Hussars)

Opposite page:
Corporal Hanley's
patrol and the
strong party of
Frenchmen,
captured at Blasco
Sancho, together
with his Military
General Service
Medal 1793–1814,
showing the
remarkable eleven
bars, and his
commemorative
silver medal
(Norwyn Photo-
graphics)

and narrowly avoided being captured. During the withdrawal from Salamanca to Ciudad-Rodrigo, the *14th* took part in picketing and other rear-guard duties until it took up positions behind the river Agueda.

On 26 May 1813, the Regiment was in the centre of the resumed Allied march on Salamanca. The *14th* and German Hussars removed the barri-cades, pushed through the town and overtook the enemy. In a short time, the line of the river Douro was won. The Allies continued with a firmness the enemy could not withstand, such was their confidence in their commander, now Marquis of Wellington. The *14th* remained in the advance-guard, and on 12 June forced an enemy division to retreat from its position near Burgos. One squadron, commanded by Captain Milles riding his horse Delpini, charged the French and took some prisoners and a gun.

Unable to withstand the British assault, the French destroyed the castle at Burgos and fell back behind the river Ebro in some confusion. The *14th* continued to lead the advance, made contact with a party of enemy at Pancorba, and on the 15th, successfully crossed the river over the bridge at Frias, 30 miles south-west of Vittoria. On 20 June, Wellington observed the enemy positions in front of the city and made his plan. Next day the battle of Vittoria was fought, and the *14th Light Dragoons* contributed to a decisive defeat of the French army. The Regiment was under Lieutenant-General Sir Rowland Hill and, with the artillery, was in support of the infantry attacks. In the after-noon it was detached to outflank the enemy's left, and in the evening pursued the rump of the French army along the road leading to Pamplona. The Regiment overtook the enemy baggage train and captured King Joseph's coach containing his silver chamber-pot later to be known as *'The Emperor'*, a cherished regimental possession to this day.

The *14th Light Dragoons* were awarded *VITTORIA* as a battle honour, and a further honorary distinction was conferred on Colonel Bathurst Hervey. While Vittoria was an important victory for the Allies, military historians claim that the success was marred by the failure to carry out a fully co-ordinated pursuit, the looting of the baggage train proving too much of a distraction. This criticism could scarcely be levelled at the *14th*. Harrying the remnant of the French army, Major Brotherton's squadron charged and captured a tumbrel. A 3-man patrol led by Lieutenant Ward captured 25 armed infantrymen at the village of Ostiz, north of Pamplona, who surrendered with some relief. On 1 July, a patrol led by Lieutenant Clavering dispersed a body of infantry of the French rear-guard on the mountain road which led across the frontier towards St-Jean-Pied-de-Port, and took eighteen prisoners. On 4 July, Major Brotherton's squadron engaged a body of the enemy and the Regiment took up outpost duties in front of Maya. The French army, reinforced and reorganised, was placed under Marshal Soult, who recommended the offensive, but without success.

On 26 July, the Regiment was responsible for bringing down the wounded from the Maya pass in the mountains. At the same time, the French were repulsed and fell back to the border. Despite the apparent reluctance to pursue after Vittoria, northern and central Spain were now virtually clear of the French who had retreated into the Pyrenees and beyond by the end of the summer. After twenty years of war, the British army was at last achieving decisive results, and the *14th Light Dragoons* had played their part in this.

On 10 November 1813, the vanguard of the Allied army were down from the mountains and into France. The *14th* were again attached to Sir Rowland Hill's Division and one squadron formed the advance-guard of Marshal Beresford's corps. The enemy position on the river Nivelle was forced, and the Regiment concentrated at Espelette to the south of Bayonne next day. Unfortunately, their baggage, still in the Pyrenees, was captured, and the three soldiers guarding it were killed. On 11 December, Major Brotherton's squadron seized a convoy of corn, wine and salt, but two days later while the Regiment was engaged elsewhere, Brotherton, Lieutenant Southwell and a trooper were taken prisoner. Brotherton's capture may well have denied him command of the *14th,* but he did command the 16th Light Dragoons and was later made Inspector-General of the Cavalry.

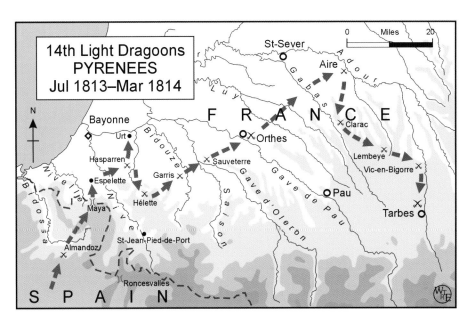

14th Light Dragoons
PYRENEES
Jul 1813–Mar 1814

On 14 December, the *14th* resumed outpost duties in front of Urt, to the east of Bayonne. During the severe winter, the army spent a period in barracks until operations were resumed in February 1814. The *14th* formed the vanguard in the advance against the enemy's left flank, leading to the actions at Hélette, Garris and Sauveterre-de-Béarn.

On 27 February the battle of Orthes was fought, and the *14th* continued to operate against the enemy's left, passing the stream above Orthes and advancing towards the main road running north-east to St-Sever. But following heavy French artillery fire, when several men and horses were wounded, they were ordered to withdraw. Fighting continued all day until the French were overpowered and driven from the field. The *14th* were awarded another battle honour: *ORTHES*, and Colonel Bathurst Hervey was rewarded with yet another honorary distinction.

The *14th* followed up a disorderly French retreat, crossed the river Adour and assisted in driving them out of Aire, where Sergeant Vernor, Privates Craig and Rose particularly distinguished themselves. On 7 March, Major-General Fane led a cavalry brigade to Pau to disrupt an attempt by Marshal Soult to arrest a party of French noblemen who were supporters of the House of Bourbon. Next day a patrol under Captain John Townsend, in support of this action, made contact with the enemy, but Townsend and four soldiers were captured.

On 13 March, the French sent a cavalry brigade to Clarac to turn the Allied right flank. The *14th* picket repulsed the attack, but Captain Babington was taken prisoner. On the 15th another picket, under Captain Badcock, was attacked by the entire 5th Regiment of Chasseurs. Reinforcement by the squadrons of Captain Milles and Captain Anderson arrived immediately, and the French were driven back with losses. After this action Captain Milles was promoted to Brevet Major.

From 16 to 20 March, the Regiment was involved in successful engagements at Lembeye, Vic-en-Bigorre and Tarbes; Lieutenant Lyons was killed. The *14th* then assumed outpost duty before advancing towards Toulouse on 22 March. At the battle of Toulouse on 10 April 1814, the Regiment was again under the command of Lieutenant-General Sir Rowland Hill, and the ensuing operations drove the French army from its ground. Hostilities were ended for the time being, Napoleon abdicated, and the Bourbons returned briefly to the French throne.

By the end of the Peninsular campaign the *14th Light Dragoons* had acquired an enviable reputation. The Regiment had become renowned for the *esprit-de-corps* between all ranks, and for the style in which officers and soldiers carried out the

Left: 'The Emperor' as it could have been found (Steve Day; courtesy The King's Royal Hussars)

Inset: Detail of the crest on 'The Emperor' (Steve Day; courtesy The King's Royal Hussars)

Left: The decorations and medals of Colonel Sir Felton Bathurst Hervey, Bt. (Courtesy Sir John Hervey-Bathurst, Bt.)

Right: Light Dragoons 1815 – privates in the 14th Light Dragoons

duties of pickets, patrols, vedettes and other outpost duties. It was awarded eight battle honours, two more than any other cavalry regiment.

In May 1814, the *14th* marched first to Bordeaux, where they were complimented on their appearance and efficiency by Major-General Lord Dalhousie, and then to Calais. They landed at Dover on 17 July, marched to London and were reviewed by the Duke of York, the now estranged husband of the royal patroness; he complimented Colonel Bathurst Hervey on the bearing of his troops, saying: 'They appear as if they had never been on service.' The Regiment then marched to the depot at Weymouth.

Right: Peninsula guidon of the 14th King's Light Dragoons (Norwyn Photographics)

Two years earlier, on 19 June 1812, the United States Congress had declared war on Great Britain, partly as a consequence of the Royal Navy's policy of seizing merchantmen trading between France and the USA, and particularly the impressment of US seamen. In mid-December 1814 a British fleet landed 7,500 troops under Major-General Sir Edward Pakenham (Wellington's brother-in-law) in a bay to the east of New Orleans, to form the southern prong of an intended triple offensive against the Americans.

Two dismounted squadrons of the *14th* had arrived in Jamaica a month earlier and were attached to Major-General Keane's force sailing to join Pakenham. After a difficult passage across the Gulf of Mexico they reached the Louisiana coast on 10

December. New Orleans was defended by General Andrew Jackson (possibly the best of a largely mediocre collection of US generals; later to become President of the USA), with about 3,000 troops.

On 8 January 1815, unaware that the signing of the Peace of Ghent on 24 December 1814 had ended the war (another squadron of the *14th* had embarked for America on 2 January), Pakenham launched a futile frontal attack with 5,000 men. Within the space of thirty minutes 2,100 of them had been killed or wounded and 500 taken prisoner. Pakenham himself was killed as were his two senior subordinates, and Major-General Keane was severely wounded. The Americans lost eight men killed and thirteen wounded. Major-General Lambert, who had now assumed command, commended the two *14th*

squadrons, and the command exercised by Lieutenant-Colonel Baker and previously that of Major Milles. Theforce re-embarked for England, but a boat carrying two officers and forty men of the *14th* was captured by the Americans.

By 16 May 1815 the Regiment had concentrated at Hounslow. During the year, the *14th Light Dragoons* were awarded the battle honour *PENINSULA*, in recognition of its services in Portugal, Spain and France.

In March 1815, Napoleon escaped from Elba and determined to resume his imperial role. The Allies mobilised once again, but only a quarter of Wellington's force of 68,000 had served under him in the Peninsula. Many of the veterans of the campaign including the *14th* were in America and to their lasting disappointment were unavailable for the Battle of Waterloo. However Colonel Felton Bathurst Hervey and Major the Hon. Henry Percy were both on Wellington's staff, the latter carrying the dispatch, reporting the Victory of 18 June 1815, to the Secretary of State for War in London.

In April 1815, the *20th* were awarded the battle honour *PENINSULA*, and they too missed the Battle of Waterloo, being in Malta at the time. In August they embarked for England and eventually concentrated at Hounslow. In July 1816, the Regiment marched to Bristol with detachments sent to other towns in Gloucestershire and in Wales for duties in support of the civil power. In March 1817, they were sent to southern Ireland, with detachments in Tipperary and adjacent counties. However, in December 1818, despite a distinguished period of service, the *20th Light Dragoons* were disbanded for the third time.

The *14th* had been sent to Cork in December 1816, and were to remain in Ireland for the next three years. On 24 September 1819, Colonel Sir Felton Bathurst Hervey, Bt, died aged 37. He had been rewarded with a baronetcy for his

Above: Peninsula guidon of the 20th Light Dragoons (Norwyn Photographics)

services in 1818 and received the many decorations illustrated on page 38. In 1813 the officers of the *14th Light Dragoons* had presented him with a sword which is now on display in *The King's Royal Hussars* barracks. In the 277-year annals of the *14th/20th King's Hussars*, Bathurst Hervey must surely have been the Regiment's bravest and most distinguished commanding officer. It was a misfortune for both the Regiment and the Army that he died so young.

Lieutenant-Colonel Charles Baker now assumed command, which he held for the next ten years. The Regiment remained in England until April 1825 when it was sent to Ireland where it remained for three years. On 26 March 1828, the *14th* returned via Liverpool and marched to Coventry and Birmingham. On 16 April 1829, Lieutenant-Colonel John Townsend, another veteran of the Peninsula and New Orleans, and who had joined the *14th* as a Cornet, succeeded Baker in command of the Regiment, which then moved to Leeds, Burnley and Rochdale and, a year later, to Brighton and Chichester.

Below: Lieutenant-Colonel John Townsend (Norwyn Photographics)

On 19 June 1830, Lieutenant-General Sir John Vandeleur made his farewell inspection as Colonel of the Regiment. He gave an enviable report on turn-out, drill, state of the barracks and condition of the horses, which he passed to the Commander-in-Chief. Although he was the Colonel, he was also a most experienced cavalry commander; having commanded the 19th Light Dragoons in 1807, a cavalry brigade throughout the Peninsular campaign and the 4th Cavalry Brigade at the Battle of Waterloo. His report on the *14th* was therefore unlikely to have been over generous.

On 26 July 1830, the Regiment was inspected by King William IV who expressed his approval of its turn-out and ordered that it should in future bear the title: *The 14th, or The King's, Regiment of Light Dragoons*. Following the new title, in 1831 the uniform was changed from blue to scarlet, and the facings from orange to blue. However, the change was not fully implemented for a while.

6

THE SECOND SIKH WAR
AND INDIAN MUTINY

The Army was often needed to maintain law and order at home, and the mobility of cavalry made them well suited to the task. Magistrates preferred regular troops rather than Yeomanry whose local connections could put a strain on their impartiality, and who were even alleged to support the Tories. In the nineteenth century, there were many civil disturbances because of poverty and unemployment. In 1819, the predecessors of the *Duke of Lancaster's Own Yeomanry* were involved in what later became known as the Peterloo Massacre in Manchester.

In October 1831 the *14th King's Light Dragoons* were based at Gloucester when serious rioting broke out in Bristol, and they were ordered to assist in restoring order. During two days of rioting which began on the 29th, mobs caused considerable damage, homes and offices were gutted, including the Customs House. On the 31st Major William Beckwith's squadron dispersed a mob plundering the cellars of the Bishop's palace, moved on to Queen's Square and finally rode through the quays and wharves. This timely action by Beckwith's men led to the rapid restoration of calm in Bristol. After this, however, they were referred to by the local populace as 'The Bloody Blues' because of the ruthlessness of the troops, still in their blue uniforms, having not yet changed to their scarlet dress.

In June 1832, the Regiment moved to Hounslow for Royal escort duties. At the same time, the King's Crest was authorised to be borne, and the *Prussian Eagle* to remain on the second and third quarters of the Guidon. Two years later, however, the

Below: 14th Light Dragoon sergeant in Summer Dress, 1831

Below right: 14th Light Dragoons group in 1836

King commanded that the use of Guidons in light dragoon regiments was to cease. The Peninsula Guidons of the *14th* did not see light of day again until they were trooped at Catterick in 1950. From March 1833, the Regiment was stationed in Ireland for three years, and on return, moved through Scotland and England until 1841 when it embarked for India.

At this time, much of India was controlled by the British East India Company from its bases in Bombay, Madras and Calcutta. The British army was needed to support the Company's troops and was frequently in action against the warring tribes. For this role, the Regiment relieved the 4th Light

Dragoons, and on 30 April 1841 Major William Havelock transferred from that regiment, as the second Lieutenant-Colonel. The Regiment sailed from Gravesend, under Lieutenant-Colonel John Townsend. On arrival in Bombay, it marched to Kirkee and remained there for three years. In October 1844, two squadrons were sent on active service to Kolapore in the southern Maratha country. Sadly, on 22 April 1845, Lieutenant-Colonel John Townsend, the commanding officer, died while on leave at his home in Ireland. Lieutenant-Colonel William Havelock succeeded him in command.

While at Kirkee, the Regiment was inspected at least twice a year, rather more than is the case today. After the last review, the Commander-in-Chief at Bombay

Above: Privates, *14th Light Dragoons in 1841, back in blue uniforms*

Below: *14th Light Dragoons after their arrival in India in 1842* (Steve Day; courtesy The King's Royal Hussars)

reported the *14th (King's) Light Dragoons* to be 'in as high a state of efficiency as any regiment in Her Majesty's service'. Like many cavalry regiments, the *14th* could be unorthodox about dress, and after their arrival in India, they wore a *puggree*, which was a length of cloth wound round the forage cap as protection against the heat, hence the Indians nicknamed them 'Puggree Wallahs'. At the end of the year, the Regiment left in good spirits for Mhow and Agra. When the First Sikh War ended in 1846, the

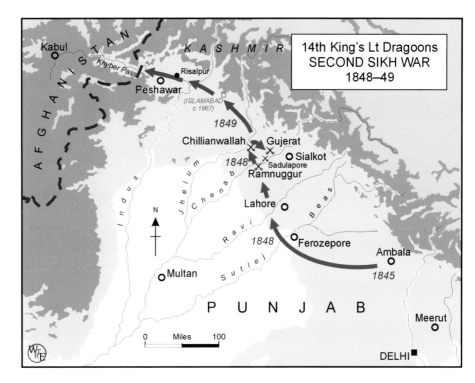

14th moved to Meerut and then Amballa until February 1848. The Left Wing, under Major John King, was then sent into action at Lahore over the river Ravi, and captured sixty Sikhs.

In November 1848, the Second Sikh War began and General Sir Hugh Gough, C-in-C India, assembled his army at Ferozepore. He sent a covering force across the river Sutlej to block any advance on Lahore where the *14th* had left a rear party with the regimental baggage and families. The covering force included the *14th Light Dragoons*, East India Company troops and artillery, reinforced by two infantry brigades. This force was initially under the command of Brigadier-General Charles Cureton, who had begun his military career as a private in Brotherton's troop during the Peninsular War, but on 8 November, General Sir Colin Campbell took over command of the covering force. The Sikhs, including their irregular cavalry known as 'Gorchurras', were about 16,000 strong with 28 guns. They held positions on both sides of the river Chenab at *Ramnuggur*, today called Rasulnagar and in Pakistan.

Campbell ordered the advance, and the 3rd Light Dragoons, supported by horse artillery, drove in the enemy outposts south of the Chenab. During this preliminary action one of the guns became bogged in quicksands at the edge of the main riverbed. The C-in-C then ordered Lieutenant-Colonel William Havelock to advance. As a fair-haired youth, Havelock had cut a dashing figure in the Peninsular War, serving with Spanish irregulars who called him 'El Chico Blanco'. This nickname stimulated his thirst for action and the order was just what he was waiting for to 'win his golden spurs' with the *14th*.

Above: Brigadier-General Charles Cureton, killed commanding the Cavalry at Ramnuggur (Norwyn Photographics)

He led off with two squadrons at a gallop towards the Sikh cavalry reserve, which was covered by fire from the Sikh main body on the north bank. The 5th Native Cavalry followed in support. Cureton, who was now reputed to be the ablest cavalry commander in India, saw that Havelock was heading for trouble and galloped up to stop him, but was shot through the head and heart. With his death the cavalry lost a superb general who would have been sorely needed at Chillianwalla the following year. However the advance continued under sustained enemy fire, though there were few casualties at first when the Regiment was at the gallop. This changed when the *14th* reached the bank of the river. When the Charge was sounded, it was impossible to comply effectively because the going had become so heavy, but the Sikhs were nevertheless cut down and driven back across the river in some confusion.

Havelock re-formed the Regiment and took the 5th Native Cavalry under command; with many of the enemy in front, he was determined to maximise his advantage. The *14th* therefore charged again into the centre of the position and successfully drove the Sikhs back, despite being exposed to murderous fire from many sides. Both regiments fought bravely but the casualties were heavy. The *14th* lost six officers, 44 men and 56 horses killed, wounded or missing, and the 5th Cavalry similarly. The casualties included Havelock, whose mutilated body was found twelve days later, with nine of his soldiers' bodies heaped on it, proving that they had tried to protect their colonel to the last. Viscount Gough wrote approvingly in his official dispatch the following day, and the engagement was also favourably reported in *The Illustrated London News*.

Despite these plaudits, the action was considered to be a purely cavalry fight, so *Ramnuggur* was not awarded as a battle honour. But it was agreed that the charges by the *14th Light Dragoons* and the 5th Light Cavalry deserved a high place among similar attacks delivered under unfavourable circumstances. The events of 22 November 1848 remain very important to those who have ever served in the Regiment. On its anniversary, 115 years later, a very different event was to happen in

Below: The Battle of Ramnuggur, by Henry Martens. Havelock is depicted at **1***, Cureton at* **2***.*

Right: *Lieutenant-Colonel William Havelock, killed leading the 14th Light Dragoons at Ramnuggur*

Far right: *his grave and memorial at Ramnuggur*

Below: *The Ramnuggur Cup, presented to the Sergeants' Mess by the 5th Light Cavalry (Steve Day; courtesy The King's Royal Hussars)*

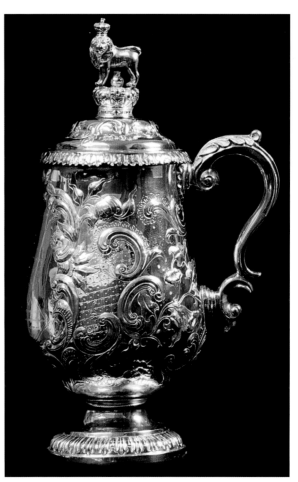

America, which would shock the whole world.

After the Indian Mutiny, the 5th Light Cavalry presented the Sergeants' Mess with the Ramnuggur Cup on which was engraved the 28 actions in which the 14th had participated since the start of the Peninsular War. The battle is still celebrated annually in the Warrant Officers' and Sergeants' Mess, and the Cup is passed round for all members and guests to drink to 'The Heroes of Ramnuggur'.

On 23 November, Lieutenant-Colonel John King assumed command and was subsequently awarded a Companionship of the Order of the Bath (CB). On 3 December the Regiment took part in an action at Sadulapore, a month before the ill-fated battle of Chillianwalla. On 13 January 1849, the *14th* were in the 2nd Cavalry Brigade with the 9th Lancers, 1st and 6th Regiments of Light Cavalry. The brigade commander was Brigadier Alexander Pope who, although having had previous good operational service as a squadron leader, was both inexperienced in such a command and ill; these shortcomings were to cause serious problems. Gough's intention was to attack the next morning, but an unexpected Sikh artillery barrage forced him to do this immediately. Extensive use of cavalry was not possible, as the country was so close. The Sikhs with 60,000 men and more than 60 guns, had a large numerical advantage and outflanked the British at both ends. The 1st Cavalry Brigade, under Brigadier White, was on the left of the line; Pope's 2nd Cavalry Brigade was on the right.

As the infantry advanced, some 800 Sikh cavalry attempted to turn the British left flank, held by White's brigade. The Sikhs were stopped, but at the expense of heavy casualties, particularly from the 3rd Light Dragoons who fought most gallantly. On the right flank the situation was less happy. Pope initially held the Sikh cavalry on his extreme right with two squadrons of the 9th Lancers, but as the infantry on his left advanced, he ordered his force, including the *14th*, to deploy. This they did in line with ten guns between them and the infantry. Pope led the brigade at the trot, but this dwindled to a walk, and this manoeuvre got into difficulty. When the Sikh horsemen appeared, the centre halted followed by the two flanks. Colonel John King galloped up to the Brigadier to persuade him to attack, but Pope did not give the order. The Sikhs charged the centre of the line and the cry: *'Threes about!'* was heard; this meant 'Retreat'. The native cavalry turned, followed by the rest of the brigade, including the *14th*, all of whom withdrew in some confusion.

The infantry and the 1st Cavalry Brigade fought well, but the premature retirement of Pope's brigade caused the battle to degenerate into a scrappy affair, with an inconclusive outcome. Had the 2nd Cavalry Brigade not pulled back as it did, Chillianwalla would have been a victory. Its memory was to haunt the *14th*, and later to lead to tragedy; blame for the débâcle must also lie with whomsoever appointed Pope to this command. At the start of the battle he was so ill that he had to be lifted into the saddle, and during the engagement he had to be evacuated because of his wounds. The *14th* losses included Lieutenant Augustus Cureton, the son of Brigadier Charles Cureton.

Below: The Battle of Chillianwalla, 13 January 1849 (National Army Museum)

Above: The Battle of Gujerat, 21 February 1849 (Steve Day; courtesy The King's Royal Hussars)

On 21 February 1849, the battle of Gujerat was fought, north of the river Chenab, after Gough's army had been reinforced with 20,000 men and 88 guns. The Sikhs were in the open, south of the town, with between 35,000 and 60,000 men but only 59 guns. After a heavy artillery barrage which lasted more than two hours and virtually silenced the Sikh artillery, the infantry broke the Sikh centre and the Sikhs withdrew. The *14th* were in the 2nd Cavalry Brigade, with 1st Light Cavalry and 11th Irregular Cavalry under Brigadier Lockwood. Warner's Troop of Horse Artillery was in support. The Brigade's task was to protect the right flank. Despite Sikh efforts to turn it, the brigade held firm and pursued the enemy for fifteen miles. During the pursuit, many enemy infantry were shot, and Corporal William Pain, of the *14th*, captured a red silk standard and killed the standard-bearer.

After the battle, the brigade and divisional commanders commended the conduct of the *14th* and their commanding officer, Lieutenant-Colonel John King. British losses at Gujerat were light, but the Sikhs had sustained 15–20,000 casualties. Their army was shattered, the victory was a triumph for Gough, and effectively ended the Second Sikh War. The Regiment was recognised on 14 December 1852 when *PUNJAUB*, *CHILLIANWALLAH*, and *GOOJERAT* were awarded as battle honours.

The *14th* then took part in the pursuit over the river Jhelum to Peshawar, and the Afghans were expelled beyond the Khyber Pass. On 2 April 1849 the Punjab was annexed to the Crown. In May the Regiment was back in Lahore where it remained for nearly two years, but the legacy of Chillianwalla remained. Sir Charles Napier replaced Gough, and reviewed the *14th Light Dragoons* in July 1850. Addressing the Regiment, he said: 'Fourteenth King's Own, I am proud to see you … and if you had

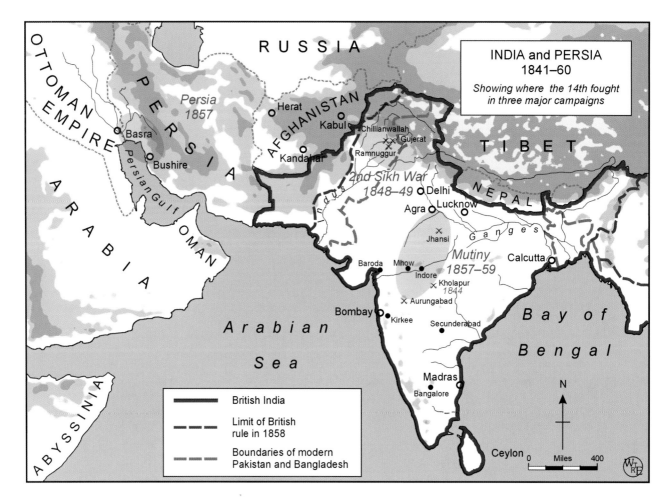

been properly handled on the thirteenth of January the disgrace that now hangs over the Regiment could not have taken place.' Such criticism would hardly have been made in public, and in front of the Regiment, if it had been aimed at the commanding officer, who had after all tried unsuccessfully to get Brigadier Pope to attack.

The accusation, however unfair, was too much for King, and he retired from the field of inspection and shot himself. While King may have lacked Havelock's panache, he had led the Left Wing well earlier and had fought bravely at Gujerat. He was, however, a man of principle, who did not subscribe to today's blame culture, which he could have done with some justification. Nevertheless, Chillianwalla was not the Regiment's proudest moment, as Kipling's poem 'Belts' suggests.*

After King's death, Lieutenant-Colonel Henry Doherty assumed command. Doherty had joined the *14th* as a cornet in 1833 and served throughout the Second Sikh War. He commanded the Regiment from 1850 to 1857, was promoted to Major-General in 1863, and to General in 1877.

On 6 March 1851, the *14th* arrived at Meerut and remained there for four years, continuing to enjoy its frequent and regular inspections. In January 1855 they were told off to join an expeditionary force that was in preparation to counter a Persian

Above: *Colonel Henry Doherty*

* 'There was a row in Silver Street that's near to Dublin Quay,
  between an Irish regiment an' English cavalree; –
  they called us "Delhi Rebels", an' we answered "Threes about!"'

army threatening Herat, the now well-known border town in Afghanistan on the north-west frontier. The Regiment marched the 900 miles from Meerut to Kirkee where they arrived on 21 April, two men dying on the march. Herat was occupied by the Shah's forces and formally annexed in October 1856.

The *14th* remained at Kirkee until 20 February 1857 when they left for Persia, under Colonel Charles Steuart, reaching Bushire in the Persian Gulf in March. Their divisional commander was Brigadier-General Henry Havelock, younger brother of Lieutenant-Colonel William Havelock. Captain Richard Prettejohn's troop accompanied a force under Lieutenant-General Sir James Outram up the Persian Gulf to Shatt-al-Arab in the Euphrates delta. Several of the troop transports were grounded so the operation got off to a slow start. The first opposition was encountered from the forts at Mohamrah on the river Karun where the Persian army was drawn up. Captain Young of the Indian Navy with four armed steamers bombarded the enemy positions, which led to a rapid Persian withdrawal. Mohamrah was captured on 26 March and Captain Prettejohn's troop was part of this successful operation. The troop returned to Bushire after the battle, and everyone was back in Kirkee in May. Despite the Regiment's relatively modest contribution to the campaign, it was awarded *PERSIA* as a battle honour.

THE INDIAN MUTINY, 1857–58

Below: An action during the Indian Mutiny in 1857 (Steve Day; courtesy The King's Royal Hussars)

Religious disquiet, and disaffection with East India Company rule among those who had been dispossessed by it lay at the heart of the growing unease that was to lead to the explosion of violence in northern India, and the British authorities unwittingly prepared the way. The number of Sepoy (Indians employed as soldiers under British discipline) units was increased, while the number of European units declined because of the demands of the Crimean War. In 1856, when Lord Canning

was appointed Governor-General, he added a truly deft touch to the situation by a decree that from now on the Bengal Army's Sepoy units would be liable for service overseas, which meant that Hindus would lose caste. The Muslim troops, meanwhile, were being subjected to propaganda by agitators who wished to restore the Moghul dynasty. A curious factor which added to the unease of the Sepoys was the circulation of *chuppaties* (Indian loaves of unleavened bread) throughout northern India. No one knew whence they came but they had to be passed on; they were thought to be a sign of impending apocalypse.

The catalyst for the mutiny was the issue of the new Enfield rifle to the Sepoys (Indians employed as soldiers under British discipline). The cartridges for this weapon had to be put in the mouth and the end bitten off before loading, and it was widely rumoured that the grease which covered them had

been deliberately made from both pig fat, unclean to Muslims, and cow fat; the Hindus regarded the cow as sacred. True or false, official assurances that these fears were groundless did nothing to calm the situation. The authorities were probably unaware that some of these troops if they believed themselves polluted would be obliged to undergo protracted purification rites, during which they were forbidden to sleep with their wives.

The first mutinous incidents were isolated and the troops involved were disarmed and disbanded. Then, on 24 April 1857, 85 men of the 3rd Bengal Cavalry at Meerut refused to touch the new cartridges. They were imprisoned, but on 10 May the Sepoys of the garrison released them and began to murder European officers and civilians. By July, the Regiment had taken the field.

The first action by the Left Wing was against the mutinous garrison at Aurungabad on 23 June. When the column under General Woodburn arrived, all the mutineers handed over their arms, apart from a troop of the 1st Native Cavalry, most of whom ran away. Some were captured, convicted of attempted assassination and hanged next morning. On 27 July, the northward march continued, the *14th* having to swim across the river Narbada near Hoshangabad on 1 August. The onset of the monsoon suspended operations for three months. On 20 October the Malwa Field Force, under Brigadier C. S. Stuart, not to be confused with Brigadier Charles Steuart of the *14th*, advanced to clear the rebels from the surrounding districts and went into action at Dhar on the 22nd. The Regiment captured three guns and three standards, while supporting the 25th Bombay Native Infantry, and Captain Richard Gall with his troop held the left flank during the charge. The enemy lost 40 men and retreated into the fort; Sergeant Gardiner's section killed several members of an ambush party, and Troop Sergeant-Major Grainger, although wounded, cut down two rebel horsemen. The fort was taken on 31 October.

On 21 November, while at breakfast, the 25th Bombay Light Infantry's position was attacked by 300 rebels. Lieutenant George Dew and his picket of the *14th Light Dragoons* charged and routed them. His personal bravery was such that he was recommended for the Victoria Cross, and several other men of the *14th* were commended for gallantry. Later that month, Captain Gall led the *14th* on operations at Goraria. Lieutenant Martin, of the Bengal Cavalry, led nineteen troopers of the *14th*, and a battery of guns, gallantly through a deep cutting into the middle of the rebel position, but he was severely wounded. Gall's squadron came to the rescue, capturing five guns and cutting up 200 rebel infantry who retired into the village. Meanwhile a force of 2,000 rebels had attacked the rear-guard of the column. Lieutenant Leonard Redmayne led a valiant charge, but was killed, and Private O'Neill also fought most bravely despite being shot through the chest, though happily he recovered. Overnight, the *14th* and other cavalry surrounded Goraria, heavy artillery was brought to bear on the village in the morning, and in the afternoon it was stormed and set ablaze. By 25 November the battle was over. Martin was mentioned in dispatches, and Gall was promoted to brevet-major.

Below: India Camp Scene, 1858 (Steve Day; courtesy The King's Royal Hussars)

In January 1858, the Regiment was split between two brigades. The Left Wing, under Major Gall, was in the 1st Brigade at Mhow, commanded by Brigadier C. S. Stuart. The Right Wing and Regimental Headquarters, under Major Arthur Scuda- more, was in the 2nd Brigade at Sehore, commanded by Brigadier Charles Steuart, *14th Light Dragoons*. During a 3-weeks' break, the official agent, Colonel Durand, wrote to Lord Canning commending the *14th* and the leadership of Gall for 'quelling this insurrection'.

The year 1858 was to be eventful, and the Regiment was to live up to its label *'The Fighting Fourteenth'*, acquired fifty years before in the Peninsula. On 8 January, Major-General Sir Hugh Rose, commanding the Central India Field Force, escorted by a troop of the *14th*, visited the 2nd Brigade when Steuart had just been awarded the CB, for the Persian campaign. On his arrival, Rose presided at a drumhead court-martial, at which 150 rebels were convicted and then shot.

On 26 January, Rose laid siege to Rathgur fort, which was strongly held and in a commanding position. After a breach had been made, the Rajah of Banpur's forces counter-attacked at the rear. Rose increased his fire and sent a small force, including a detachment of *14th*, to drive away the new threat; the enemy withdrew rapidly, throwing away their arms and ammunition. During the night of the 28th, the rebels evacuated the fort and took up positions near Barodia. At 4 p.m. on 30 January, Rose attacked, forced a crossing over the Bina river, and the rebels were defeated.

The Rajah escaped, but the country south of Saugor was now clear of rebels, and the road from Indore could be used for the relief of Saugor. Another happy outcome was that the charger of Lieutenant Redmayne, killed at Goraria, was recovered and was purchased by General Rose. Saugor was finally relieved on 3 February, having survived a 7-month siege during which its defenders, the 31st Bengal Infantry had remained steadfastly loyal under their Indian officers. Captain William McMahon's troop of the *14th* with two native companies remained behind to defend it while the

Below: Campaign in Central India, 1858 (Steve Day; courtesy The King's Royal Hussars)

field force advanced to Garrakota. On arrival, Rose put down an effective bombardment, which put the rebel garrison to flight. Next day, a mixed force, including the troops of Captains Robert Brown and Arthur Need, killed nearly 100 enemy, of whom Need personally accounted for five. General Rose recommended him for a mention in dispatches. Rose's next objective was Jhansi, approached through the mountain passes of Malthone and Muddenpore. The latter was forced on 4 March after Major Scudamore's squadron successfully created a diversion in the Malthone pass.

In the meantime, the Left Wing of the *14th*, under Major Richard Gall, had left Mhow on 10 January with the 1st Brigade of the Central India Field Force. They marched 70 miles up the Agra road to Chandri, where they were confronted by a strongly held rebel position. Gall went forward to reconnoitre through thick jungle and came under fire. Next day the infantry advanced with artillery support, and the forward position was taken. During the week the surrounding villages were cleared, and on the night of 16/17 March Lieutenant Patrick Gowan's troop made a successful feint, firing blank ammunition. Next day Chandri fort was taken, all the guns and substantial supplies falling into British hands. On the 19th the Left Wing, under Gall, marched the 70 miles to Jhansi in three days, to rejoin the Right Wing.

Jhansi lay at the heart of the rebellion in Central India, so its capture was of vital importance. It was held by probably the most unusual military commander of the nineteenth century, the 30-year-old Rani Lakshmi Bai, who was literate, politically skilful and an accomplished swordswoman. She had been loyal to the British even during the early stages of the Mutiny. In 1857 the British inhabitants of Jhansi were murdered by the mutineers and she had paid them to leave the city. When she reported the massacre to the British she was suspected of complicity, so she mustered an army to hold the place.

By 22 March, the 2nd Cavalry Brigade, under Brigadier Steuart, which included the *14th*, had completed the encirclement of the city. The siege lasted seventeen days, firing from both sides being incessant, but the rebels could not escape. During the whole time, men never took off their clothes and the horses were always bridled except to be fed and watered, but morale was high. Because the brigade had only two 'eighteen-inch' guns to demolish the massive walls, a breach was not effected until 31 March, which coincided with the unexpected arrival of 22,000 mutineers and 28 guns led by Tantia Topi. He was possibly the best of the rebel leaders and had played a leading role in the massacre at Cawnpore.

This new threat demanded that Rose find an immediate reserve. He formed this with detachments from 1st Brigade, under Stuart, and from 2nd Brigade which he led himself. At 4 a.m. Topi advanced, but Rose took immediate action. He placed a field battery and Captain Richard Prettejohn's squadron of the *14th* on his left with orders to attack the enemy's right. He placed his heavy guns and infantry in the centre. He sent 1st Brigade to the far left to deny access to Jhansi over the river fords. Rose himself commanded the right of the line with Captain Arthur Need's troop of the *14th*, a troop of the Nizam's Cavalry and a horse artillery troop, with orders to attack the enemy's left. Despite the steady enemy advance and sustained fire, the effective use of artillery, the surprise charge of the infantry from the centre and the decisive cavalry charges, the battle turned favourably. Rose personally led Need's troop into the enemy's left, while Prettejohn, McMahon and Dew led their troops against the right. The charge led (unusually) by the

General, presumably on Redmayne's horse, with the bareheaded Captain Prettejohn, changed likely defeat into a victory which cost the enemy 1,500 men.

On the far left, Brigadier Stuart cut off a further enemy advance to Jhansi, and Lieutenant James Giles's troop of the *14th* distinguished themselves by cutting up a large number of enemy. Seeing that the day was lost, Tantia Topi set the adjacent jungle ablaze and under cover of the smoke withdrew his reserve over the river Betwa. Captains Need and Prettejohn led their troops at the head of the *14th* at the gallop through the burning jungle; eighteen guns, two standards and large quantities of ammunition were captured. Rose halted the pursuit when the cavalry were a mile and a half beyond the river.

During this action at the Betwa on 1 April 1858, Captain Need raced up through some rocks, had his jacket, saddle and reins cut and was isolated from his troop. However, in an act of great bravery and devotion, Lieutenant James Leith charged alone and rescued him; he was awarded the Victoria Cross. Leith was also mentioned in a dispatch, as were Captains Need and Prettejohn, and Sergeant Gardiner. The *14th* lost five men killed and 25 wounded at Betwa, the heaviest casualties of any regiment engaged.

Although the action at Betwa was fought essentially by the Reserve from the Central India Field Force, the main body meanwhile were by no means idle. The Jhansi garrison were continuing to fire on the besiegers, though they made no attempt to escape, perhaps because of the diversionary attack by Gall's squadron on part of the city wall. On 3 April Rose launched his main attack on the fort. It started with another feint by Gall, then the walls were stormed by infantry and engineers at two points with the two brigadiers commanding the reserves. The left attack was successful but on the right, there were some serious casualties among the Bombay Engineers. While the attack was in progress, Gall led a mixed detachment to storm a position held by 400 escaped rebels who were killed.

Left: Lieutenant James Leith, VC. The exploit for which he was awarded the medal was the rescue of Captain Arthur Need at Betwa on 1 April 1858, shown far left (Norwyn Photographics)

The fortress was finally occupied on 5 April, but at some cost; British losses were 343 killed and wounded including 36 officers. While 1,000 enemy bodies were counted, it was estimated that 5,000 rebels were casualties. Rose noted that the Rani's father was caught during a breakout and hanged immediately. In mopping-up operations after the city had fallen, Gall commanded a detachment which cut up or shot some 600 rebels.

After Jhansi was taken, the next objective was Kalpi. On 22 April, Gall, now a Brevet Lieutenant-Colonel, led a column north-east to Pooch on the Kalpi road. On 5 May, he personally led the storming of Lohari fort and was wounded. On 7 May, Tantia Topi moved the rebel army into positions at Koonch. After Gall had carried out a reconnaissance, the wood was cleared by infantry and the town was stormed. Captains Gordon and Thompson's troops of the *14th* played prominent parts, and the gallant charge by the former was mentioned in a dispatch by General Rose on 24 May. In Captain McMahon's squadron, Captain Blyth and Captain Prettejohn's troops charged the enemy's skirmishers magnificently despite McMahon receiving three sabre wounds. The pursuit came to a halt seven miles from Koonch, partly because of the heat, which caused many men, including the general, to suffer from heat stroke.

Despite the conditions, the *14th* were reported to be 'never better than on this day charging like demons straight into the huge masses of Sepoys'. In his dispatch, after the battle of Koonch, Rose mentioned five regimental officers for favourable consideration to the C-in-C: Captains Gordon, McMahon, Prettejohn, Todd, Brigadier Steuart's brigade-major, and Blyth.

On 10 May, the two brigades marched to Kalpi. Brigadier Steuart, unfortunately had to relinquish command of 2nd Brigade because of illness. The rear-guard of this brigade was attacked at Golowee during the night of 21/22 May, but casualties were slight. The enemy made a feint attack on the 1st Brigade at 9 a.m., which was pushed well home. Rose held firm, however, anticipating that the main attack would be on his right. His judgement was fulfilled, and it came suddenly in superior numbers and in intense heat giving the rebels an initial advantage. There were more casualties to heat stroke and, as in today's army before the SA 80 was modified, many rifles jammed. However, the Central India Field Force held firm, the attacks on both left and right having failed. The fire of the heavy guns was decisive and the fort was abandoned. The rebels suffered ten times the casualties of the British, and Kalpi was taken on 23 May. Gall led the *14th*, and Hyderabad Cavalry, with horse artillery support, in immediate pursuit, and all the enemy guns and six elephants were captured.

Rose again commended the performance of the Regiment in his final dispatch and also specially mentioned Colonel Gall for his gallant conduct in the pursuit at Golowee and Kalpi. The *14th* had been in the saddle for thirteen hours and had pursued down eight miles of road. In Gall's report of 25 May, Captains Barrett and Need, Lieutenant Giles, Regimental-Sergeant-Major Clark and Private Winton of 'B' Troop were specially mentioned for gallant services. In further charges led by Colonel Gall and Captain Smith, three guns and four elephants were captured and about 500 rebels were cut up.

Gwalior had to be reached before the monsoon, so the pursuit continued. The troops usually left their bivouac areas at 11 p.m., so as to arrive at new camp sites by sunrise; on one day the temperature reached 130° F (54° C). Nevertheless Rose force-marched the column and reached Morar, which was strongly held, on 16 June. He positioned the *14th* and the Hyderabad Cavalry on both flanks, the infantry and guns in the centre. The enemy was then driven out; the rout was completed by a wing of the *14th,* under Captain Pearson Thompson, and a further charge was made by Lieutenant Gowan's troop.

On 17 June, the Central India Field Force was reinforced from Rajputana by a column which included the 8th Hussars under Brigadier Smith. Rose took the rebels by surprise at Kotah-ki-Serai, south–east of Gwalior, and, according to the historian Philip Haythornthwaite:

> The Rani attempted to stay the flight of her troops, reputedly charging with a sword in each hand, her reins in her teeth, but was shot by a member of the 8th Hussars; she rode away but lived for only a few minutes. Her cremation ceremonies were unfinished when the 8th Hussars drove away the mourners.'

On 18 June Rose joined Smith and resumed the march on Gwalior with 1st Brigade; both columns bivouacked at the river Morar for the night. On the 19th he launched an effective infantry attack, supported by the *14th* and horse artillery, after which Brigadier Smith attacked the 'Phool Bagh' (a flower garden and palace at the foot of the fort) with horse artillery and a squadron of the *14th* who impressed him with their steadiness. Gwalior fort was taken next day in a costly attack by the 25th Bombay Native Infantry in which one of their young officers, Lieutenant Rose, died a hero's death. The new enemy commander, Tantia Topi, deserted his post at the height of battle with some rebel cavalry as guards. Squadrons of the 8th Hussars and the *14th Light Dragoons* escorted the legitimate ruler, the Prince of Gwalior, to his palace. Subsequently he presented the officers and men of the Central India Field Force with 'The Gwalior Star', an elegant silver medal with '1858' engraved upon it.

After the victory at Gwalior, Rose ordered Brigadier Napier to pursue the rebels with the 2nd Brigade. Napier's force was only 690 strong, but included a large Indian cavalry contingent and Captain Prettejohn's 62-strong troop of the *14th*. The brigade started the march in extreme heat within two hours of receiving the order. On the morning of 21 June 1858, it met 12,000 rebels under Tantia Topi, drawn up in two lines at Jowra-Alipore. Napier held the cavalry in dead ground at the front and sent his horse artillery to enfilade the enemy lines from their left flank, which tactic unnerved the mutineers who were completely routed by a cavalry charge, losing 25 guns and 300 men killed. Captains Prettejohn and Todd and Surgeon Stewart were specially mentioned in the Brigadier's dispatches. Private Novell, who charged alone into a village under heavy fire and killed one of the mutineers, was recommended for the Victoria Cross. This was a remarkable victory because the 2nd Brigade was outnumbered 17 to 1.

While this action was taking place, Major-General Sir Hugh Rose left the Central India Field Force to take command of the Poona Division of the Bombay Army. Rose has been described as the best soldier the Mutiny threw up;* Corporal George Stent,

* Harris, John. *The Indian Mutiny.*

of the *14th*, wrote that he 'would follow him to the devil'. The Regiment was exceptionally lucky to be commanded in such a demanding theatre by such an outstanding general.

The Central India Field Force was now largely broken up. Brigadier-General Charles Napier took over the Gwalior Division, which included three squadrons of the *14th*, the fourth being sent with 1st Brigade to Jhansi. Many members of the Regiment were sent home on sick leave, including Steuart, while commanding 2nd Brigade, Major Arthur Scudamore, while in acting command of the Regiment, Captain Robert Brown, Lieutenants James Leith, VC, William Travers and Veterinary-Surgeon Henry Dawson. On the departure of Scudamore, Lieutenant-Colonel Richard Gall justifiably assumed command.

When the monsoon began, a period of rest had been hoped for, but this was not to be. On 23 September, to counter a new rebel threat to Jhansi Captain Pearson Thompson led a column, which included two troops of the *14th*, in a successful action at Garotha, after which, Thompson was personally congratulated by the Viceroy of India. On 17 December, the Regiment took part in the battle of Ranode, its last action of any consequence during the Indian Mutiny. The rebel commander, Ferozshah, was advancing south along the river Scinde. Brigadier-General Napier led a force of about 350 men, including a squadron of the *14th*, under Captain Richard Prettejohn, to counter this threat. Fortunately complete surprise was achieved, and the cavalry effectively charged and pursued for eight miles. The rebels offered little resistance, though Prettejohn was dismounted by a severe sabre cut to his left thigh; which concerned him greatly because his horse galloped away with his cigars.

Below: *The Battle of Ranode, 17 December 1858* (Steve Day; courtesy The King's Royal Hussars)

After the battle, Napier wrote to Lieutenant-Colonel Gall, commending the Regiment and Prettejohn in particular. Certain officers and men of the Regiment were mentioned in dispatches: Captains Prettejohn, Need and Todd, Lieutenant Giles, Regimental-Sergeant-Major Thomas Clark and Corporal George Best. As the campaign ended for the *14th*, in recognition of their services, Majors Scudamore and Gall were promoted to Brevet Lieutenant-Colonel and appointed CBs, Captains Todd, Thompson, Prettejohn, McMahon and Need were promoted to Brevet Major. Regimental-Sergeant-Major Clark was awarded a medal for 'gallant conduct in the field'.

From January to late April 1859, much of the Regiment was detached in flying columns hunting rebels throughout the provinces. On 4 March, a warning order was received for embarkation to England. Before leaving, Brigadier-General Sir Robert Napier, the Commander of the Gwalior Division, issued a farewell order in which he commended the *14th Light Dragoons*, in enviable terms, on their performance throughout the Indian Mutiny.

On 23 May, the embarkation order to move to England was countermanded, and the Regiment returned to Kirkee, where it remained for a further nine months. Their embarkation for England from Bombay began on 11 February 1860. So ended a period of nineteen years in India and Persia, of which the *14th Light Dragoons* could be justifiably proud. Their service during the Indian Mutiny was rewarded by *CENTRAL INDIA* being awarded as a battle honour. The Regiment staged in England before sailing for Ireland. In July 1860, they were at Newbridge, under Colonel Charles Steuart, who was now fully recovered.

Left: 14th Light Dragoons Officers and Private, 1859, by R. Simkin

7 LIGHT DRAGOONS TO HUSSARS

In November 1860, Major-General William Beckwith who had so effectively suppressed the Bristol Riots as a squadron leader in 1831, became Colonel of the Regiment. In June 1861, Lieutenant-Colonel Arthur Scudamore, assumed command. On 13 August, the Commander-in-Chief, the Duke of Cambridge, reviewed the Regiment and expressed approval at what he saw, and two days later, the Prince of Wales dined with the officers and no doubt enjoyed himself.

On 17 August 1861, the *14th (King's) Light Dragoons* were converted to Hussars with the title *14th (King's) Hussars*. The uniform remained blue, but with well-defined frogging, yellow busby bags and white plumes. Apart from uniform, there were no other changes. On 26 August the Regiment took part in a review of troops by Queen Victoria in the Curragh, who said she was gratified at their appearance.

In August 1858, the rule of India had been transferred from The East India Company to the British Crown. Despite considerable opposition because of pay and conditions, known as the 'White Mutiny', the Company's armed forces were also transferred to the Crown. These included 250 volunteers from the *2nd Bengal European Light Cavalry*. On 2 May 1861, they joined the British Army as the resurrected

Below: Two 14th King's Hussars officers, in their new uniforms, being served at 'The Bell' inn (Norwyn Photographics; a painting presented to the Regimental Museum by his family in memory of Captain A. J. C. Stanton, who was killed in action on 29 January 1944)

20th Light Dragoons who had been in limbo for forty years. The commanding officer was Lieutenant-Colonel James Stannus from the 5th Bengal Light Cavalry, a veteran of Ramnuggur, Chillianwalla and Gujerat, where he was severely wounded. The second lieutenant-colonel was Edward Charles Warner, another veteran. The Regiment was redesignated *20th Hussars* and, early in 1863, marched to Sialkot in the Punjab, as trouble had once again broken out on the North-West Frontier. The *20th* were to remain there for the next seven years, protecting lines of communication.

In May 1862, the *14th* left Ireland for Manchester and Preston, staying in the north-west where they helped suppress riots at Stalybridge, and marched through other cotton towns to discourage industrial unrest. In April 1863, the Regiment left Lancashire for Aldershot. On 24 February 1866, sudden orders were received to relieve the Carabineers in London who had been sent to Ireland because of Nationalist disturbances. On 3 December, the *14th* were ordered to Wellington Barracks and the Royal Mews following riots in Hyde Park.

On 2 April 1867, the Regiment marched north and carried out spectacular fire rescues in Newcastle; every man who took part received a new uniform and an extra week's pay. The *14th* reached Edinburgh in May 1867, stayed in Scotland for a year during which they escorted Queen Victoria on her visit to Floors Castle. They also assisted the civil power during an attempted Irish Nationalist uprising in Glasgow. In May 1868 the Regiment returned to Newbridge to relieve the *10th Hussars* under the celebrated Colonel Valentine Baker, who was later to attract notoriety when he was convicted for assaulting a young lady in a railway carriage. The *14th* remained in Ireland for six years with the primary role of supporting the civil power, particularly during rowdy elections.

The *20th* remained in India until 1872 when they embarked for England where they were stationed first at Colchester and then Aldershot. On 2 May 1874, the Regiment was officially recognised as the legitimate descendant of the *20th Light Dragoons* and awarded the battle-honour: *PENINSULA*. They then spent three happy years at Brighton before moving to Leeds to help keep the peace during industrial disputes. From the north, the *20th* returned to Newbridge and deployed troops into the towns and villages nearby.

In May 1874, the *14th* left Dublin for Aldershot for a year, then moved to Colchester, before embarkation for India. This was a generally uneventful period except that during a farewell inspection by the Duke of Cambridge, it was discovered that the favoured pork chops, prepared for the Commander-in-Chief's luncheon, had been eaten by the Riding-Master. Despite this lapse in the officers' mess, which is not entirely unknown today, His Royal Highness was kind enough to express his satisfaction with the Regiment's discipline and even good conduct.

On 4 January 1876, the *14th King's Hussars* sailed from Portsmouth and disembarked at Bombay on 14 February. They moved by rail to Poona and then to Bangalore where they remained for five years. In November 1878 orders were received for active service in Afghanistan, but these were cancelled three weeks later, because unrest had developed in South Africa. In February 1881 the Regiment was ordered to South Africa to assist in crushing the Boer uprising. They sailed from

Above: Lieutenant-Colonel James Stannus, as a cornet in the 5th Bengal Light Cavalry. He transferred to the 20th Hussars, as their second commanding officer, and later became a general (Courtesy Douglas Hill)

Bombay and arrived at Durban, en route for Pietermaritzberg and Estcourt, between 14 and 26 March. Before its arrival, the Boers had encircled and defeated the relatively weak British force at Majuba Hill, after which Gladstone unwisely agreed to grant independence to the Transvaal, in accordance with his liberal – with a big and a small 'L' – views. So the First Boer War ended without the Regiment firing a single shot, and this premature conclusion was to store up trouble for the British in the future. However, after hostilities had ended, at a rifle match a team of Boers were defeated by a team of the *14th* firing at targets at known ranges;* skill at arms in the cavalry was unusual at the time, and this achievement against such doughty fighters may have been the start of the Regiment's significant shooting successes over so many years.

On 17 April, the *14th* marched to Ladysmith for an uneventful stay apart from a stampede of the horses when several were lost, drowned in the river Klip. In November the Regiment sailed back to India, having cunningly managed to sell its worst horses at high prices to the Boers. By 21 February 1882 all were concentrated at Secunderabad where they remained for more than four years. Unfortunate occurrences at Secunderabad were the sudden death from hepatitis of the commanding officer, Lieutenant-Colonel John Knox, and that of two subalterns, Lieutenants George Seymour and Dunbar Bentley-Innes, who were killed by lightning while playing billiards in the mess.

In October 1886 the Regiment under Lieutenant-Colonel Charles Morton, sailed from Bombay to Portsmouth where they entrained for a hutted camp at Shorncliffe. On 23 July 1887, the regimental shooting team won for the first time the Royal Cambridge Challenge Shield, competed for annually by cavalry regiments. On 4 June 1888, the Regiment moved to Aldershot. On 23 July they were reviewed by Field Marshal the Duke of Cambridge in Long Valley, Aldershot and on 7 August by the Kaiser.

In the meantime, Great Britain had gained control of Egypt and the Suez Canal after the victory of Lieutenant-General Sir Garnet Wolseley at Tel-el-Kebir, though a lengthy campaign was to follow. General Gordon was sent to negotiate the evacuation of the Sudan, but Khartoum was blockaded, overwhelmed in January 1885 and Gordon was killed. All British forces were therefore ordered back to Egypt. Reinforcements were needed, and two squadrons of the *20th Hussars*, under Lieutenant-Colonel C.

Below: 14th King's Hussars soldier, mounted on a grey, with his officer's charger (Steve Day; courtesy The King's Royal Hussars)

*The Marquess of Anglesea. A History of the British Cavalry, 1816–1919

Mangles, embarked in February 1885 and landed at Suakin, on the Red Sea, in March. On arrival orders were given for the neutralisation of the forces of Osman Digna, in the port area of Suakin from where Digna's slave traders operated. The first objective was the elimination of several thousand of Digna's men at Tamai, some sixty miles to the west. An armed reconnaissance towards Hagheen, led by a squadron of the *20th* engaged an outpost and put the enemy to flight. The force returned to Suakin, and the squadron re-embarked to rejoin the rest of the regiment in Cairo, by which time the last Egyptian garrison had been overwhelmed and the Sudan was abandoned. However, a British brigade continued to hold Aswan, and troops of the *20th* were sent to frontier outposts at Wadi Halfa and Korosko.

On 30 December 1886, the frontier field force, now reinforced by a British-led Egyptian brigade, advanced against the Dervishes at Ginnis to the south of Wadi

Right: 20th Hussars skewbald drum-horse, 1892. (Steve Day)

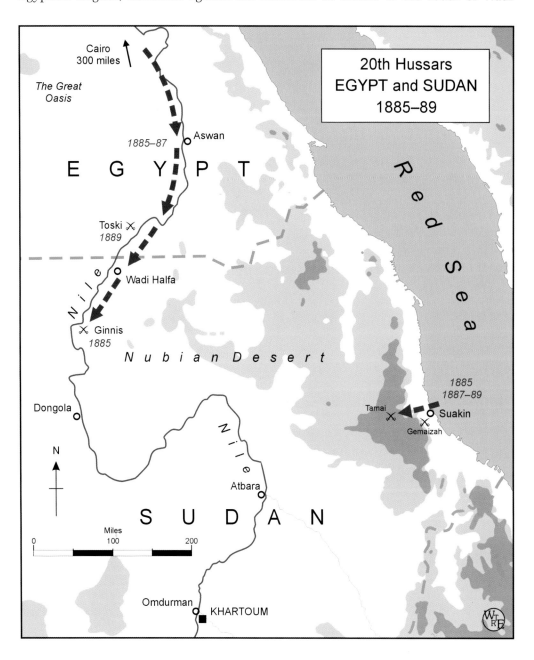

Halfa. The British advanced in line with the *20th* on the flanks. As the Dervishes broke under the infantry musketry, the Regiment wheeled and charged. In the ensuing rout the enemy lost 800 men; British losses amounted to 41. The battle, the last in which the infantry wore red coats, removed the danger of an invasion of Egypt and the *20th* left Aswan for home, apart from one squadron which returned to the still besieged Suakin. The governor of the port was Colonel (later Field Marshal) Herbert Kitchener. On 20 December 1888 he drove the Dervishes from their positions and they were subsequently charged by the *20th* at Gemaizah and put to flight, losing 500 killed and wounded. British and Egyptian casualties numbered 50, including Kitchener himself and five privates in the *20th* killed. In January 1889, after Suakin had been finally secured, the *20th* squadron returned to Cairo.

In July the Dervishes advanced once again into Egypt. The *20th*, therefore, sailed up the Nile in barges to Toski on 1 August. After a rapid disembarkation, the squadron rode out against the enemy. In an engagement lasting seven hours, the Dervishes were routed and, during a charge by the *20th*, lost more than 1,000 men including their commander, Wad-an-Nagumi. The squadron then embarked for home and rejoined the Regiment at Aldershot. *SUAKIN 1885* was awarded as a battle honour, and *VIMIERO* was transferred to the *20th Hussars* in 1890, when they were recognised as the lawful successors to the *20th Light Dragoons*.

From 1889 to 1894 the *14th*, based in the Midlands and in the south, enjoyed a number of sporting successes. On 6 June 1890, a chestnut colt, 'Sainfoin', owned by the adjutant, Captain Sir James Miller, Bt, won the Derby; the first time by a serving officer on full pay; another of his horses, 'Rocksand', was to win the St Leger in 1903. On 29 July 1890, the shooting team won the Cambridge Shield at Bisley for the second time and, in 1891, for the third time.

Below: *14th King's Hussars exercising under Colonel Henry Blackburn Hamilton in 1891 (Courtesy Colonel John Pharo-Tomlin)*

Top: The charge of the 20th Hussars at Gemaizah, as depicted by Richard Caton Woodville

Above: Sainfoin, owned by the Adjutant, Captain Sir James Miller, Bt., won the Derby in 1890 (Steve Day; courtesy The King's Royal Hussars)

On 1 April 1892, squadron organisation was formally introduced into the cavalry: 'A' and 'B' Troops became 'A' Squadron, 'C' and 'D' Troops became 'B' Squadron, 'E' and 'F' Troops became 'C' Squadron, and 'H' and 'K' Troops became 'D' Squadron. On 12 August 1892, the Regiment was based at Hulme Barracks, Manchester. A year later detachments were sent to deal with disturbances in Wales: at Newport, at Holywell and Mold, where the Chief Constable wrote that the troops' behaviour 'won the respect of all classes'.

On 21 May 1894, Queen Victoria opened the Manchester Ship Canal. The *14th* provided a Sovereign's Escort and, with the King's Liverpool Regiment, lined the route through Manchester and Salford. Afterwards the Mayor of Salford wrote: 'I was delighted to witness the smartness, good-temper and discipline which your men displayed under rather trying circumstances along the route.' During June and July the Regiment sailed from Liverpool for the south of Ireland.

Lieutenant-Colonel Miles Stapleton, who was to become Lord Beaumont, commanded the *20th Hussars* from 1891 to 1895. While in command, he secured the Queen's approval to change the colour of the plumes from crimson to yellow. In 1895 the Regiment was ordered back to India. On arrival at Bombay, the *20th* moved to Mhow by train where they took over the horses left behind by the 7th Hussars who were on their way to South Africa. They remained in India for six years.

In June 1898, the *14th* marched to the cavalry barracks in Newbridge with one squadron detached to the Curragh camp. In August they supplied escorts for the Duke and Duchess of York during the royal visit to Dublin. While there, the *14th* were generously entertained by the 13th Hussars, their comrades in arms during the Peninsular War.

In October 1899, the *14th* was placed on a war establishment and warned for active service in South Africa, but embarkation was delayed, and the Regiment moved to Aldershot because of a serious outbreak of influenza and pink-eye among the horses. Fortunately, two months later the horses were fit, and the Regiment embarked for Cape Town.

8 THE BOER WAR AND AFTERWARDS

An architect of the expanding British Empire in Africa was Cecil Rhodes, who dreamed of building a railway from Cairo to the Cape, running entirely through British territory. This idea was opposed by the Afrikaner settlers who had controlled the Transvaal and Orange Free State since 1881. The discovery of diamonds at Kimberley and gold in the Transvaal boosted the imperial appetite for these provinces, and the prospectors, called 'Uitlanders' by the locals, flocked to the mines and threatened to outnumber the Afrikaners. The Boers therefore taxed these immigrants heavily and denied them the right to vote. As a result, Rhodes organised a revolt and invasion with a view to overthrowing the Boer government. This incursion, known as the Jameson Raid, was defeated and President Kruger subsequently demanded independence for the Transvaal and the Orange Free State, which the British government refused. The Second Boer War began.

While the *14th King's Hussars* were preparing for war, Kruger's army made attacks into Natal and Cape Colony, and besieged Kimberley, Ladysmith and Mafeking. From 10 to 15 December 1899, 'Black Week', as it came to be called, the British were decisively defeated at Colenso, Magersfontein and Stormberg. The main body of the Regiment staged at Cape Town and on 6 January 1900 disembarked at Durban whence it travelled by train to Estcourt. There they joined the Royal Dragoons and the 13th Hussars in the 1st Natal Cavalry Brigade, under the overall command of General Sir Redvers Buller, prior to the relief of Ladysmith.

'B' Squadron, which had sailed later, disembarked at Cape Town on 10 January and left to join Major-General French's Cavalry Division at the Modder River. There,

Below: Major Richard Brooksbank, dressed for war in South Africa, 1899 (Norwyn Photographics)

Below right: Officers have breakfast at Estcourt (Courtesy Mrs Terence Gossage)

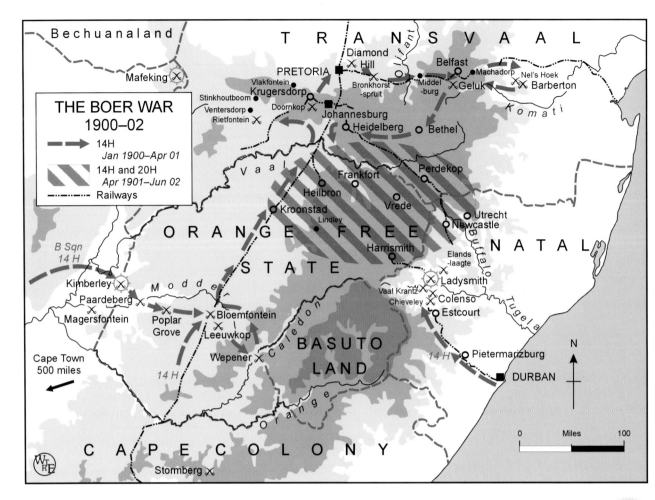

THE BOER WAR
1900–02
→ 14H
Jan 1900–Apr 01
▨ 14H and 20H
Apr 1901–Jun 02
—·—·— Railways

Kitchener, Chief of Staff to Field Marshal Lord Roberts, summoned French and his staff officer, young Douglas Haig, and told them their job was to outflank Cronje's line at Magersfontein and relieve Kimberley. This operation was remarkable in its audacity and had even been considered 'ill-advised' before the event. The Division, with 6,000 horses, in three brigades, was formed up *en masse* and covered by the fire of six RHA batteries. 'B' Squadron of the *14th* was in the 1st Cavalry Brigade with the Greys, Carabineers and one squadron of the 6th (Inniskilling) Dragoons.

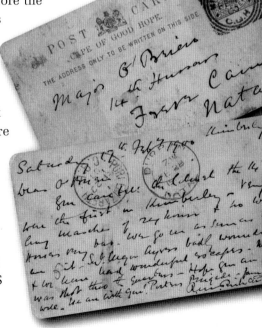

At 2 a.m. on 12 February the advance started in bright moonlight. One troop of the 16th Lancers cut the wire defences and took heavy casualties. The entire division then rode forward in column of brigades. After taking an intermediate drift, the Cavalry Division charged. 'B' Squadron *14th King's Hussars*, under Major Robert Richardson, formed the screen and was in the lead. The Boers scattered and Lieutenant Walker's troop was the first of the cavalry into Kimberley on 15 February, being met by Cecil Rhodes in person. The only regimental casualty was SQMS Ayres who was wounded in the knee.

Below: *Major-General French and his staff ride into Kimberley, led by 'B' Squadron 14th King's Hussars (Courtesy De Beers)*

Below left: *'B' Squadron Leader's account of the advance into Kimberley to the 2i/c, Major Edmund O'Brien: 'You can tell the Colonel the 14th were the first in Kimberley – Very long marches of 24 hours & no water. Horses very tired. We go on as soon as they are fit. Sgt-Major Ayres badly wounded but we have had wonderful escapades. My horse was shot thro the quarters.' R. M. Richardson (Courtesy Mrs Terence Gossage)*

This divisional cavalry charge was notable as being the only occasion during the whole campaign that infantry were successfully attacked and defeated by cavalry in force. Cavalry remained important for scouting and skirmishing, but decisive charges such as this were becoming less and less common. Nevertheless, the mounted arm still had a role to play, as was to be proved twenty years later by the *20th Hussars* in Turkey.

On 21 February, 'B' Squadron took part in the operations at Paardeberg, which led to General Cronje's surrender. On 6 March, the squadron crossed to the south of the Modder River and fought at Poplar Grove and Driefontein, and were present at the surrender of Bloemfontein.

Meanwhile Lieutenant-Colonel Gilbert Hamilton had moved RHQ and 'A' Squadron to Frere in Natal, and the Regiment was engaged at Chieveley on 15 January 1900. On the 24th the Second-in-Command, Major Edmund O'Brien, assumed command temporarily to allow the Colonel some rest. He led RHQ and 'A' Squadron, on a reconnaissance in force to Hussar Hill, north of Chieveley, in order to establish the strength of the enemy positions at Hlangwane Hill, north of Colenso. They came under heavy fire and suffered 25 casualties who included the Medical Officer, Captain Dalton. He was shot in the stomach but happily recovered. The Regiment was commended for its steadiness under fire, and Sergeant Griffin's name was specially noted.

On 5 February, RHQ, including the Maxim gun mounted on a mule, with 'A' and 'C' Squadrons took part in an unsuccessful action at Vaal Krantz. The ground denied effective cavalry movement and made them highly vulnerable to enemy fire. Buller ordered the *14th* to cover a withdrawal as the position could not be taken. The Regiment returned to Springfield on the Tugela River and took up outposts. The campaign continued in the cautious manner, which had become Buller's hallmark.

On 21 February, the 1st Natal Cavalry Brigade marched to Chieveley and Colenso, *14th* acting as rear-guard. The Regiment fought at Pieters Hill on 23 February, and

crossed the Tugela by pontoon a week later. Major O'Brien's squadron on the left and a 13th Hussars squadron on the right led the advance north, but again they were ordered to avoid casualties. On the 28th Buller's cavalry entered Ladysmith and ended the siege.

SSM Sutherland's patrol disappeared for 24 hours and successfully harassed the retreating Boers' flank. As the two leading squadrons came under fire they were ordered to withdraw, rather than exploit and inflict a reverse on the Boers. On 1 March 1900, the Brigade marched towards Ladysmith and 'C' Squadron under Major Edward Brown, covered the right flank. The *14th* led the Brigade into the town on 3 March, and were welcomed by the hungry and exhausted garrison troops who lined the streets. On the 5th the Regiment moved to Elandslaagte and made contact with the Boers until orders came to rejoin the main army at Bloemfontein. The *14th* moved by train to Durban and arrived at East London on 22 March. The Regiment was later awarded the battle honour: *RELIEF OF LADYSMITH.*

On 11 April the *14th* moved up country to Donkerhoek near Bloemfontein, having drawn remounts en route to rehorse 'A' and 'C' Squadrons. 'B' Squadron rejoined three days later, and Lieutenant-Colonel Gilbert Hamilton could now concentrate the Regiment in French's Cavalry Division in the Orange River Colony. Unfortunately, on 19 April, the 17th Lancers, while practising an advance, true to form, galloped through the *14th*'s lines. Troop horses bolted, and despite a prolonged search, the Regiment was 50 short for the relief of Wepener. The Regiment came under continual long-range rifle fire at Leeuwkop and Roodekop on 22 and 23 April. During these engagements, Captain Denny, from the King's Dragoon Guards, commanding 'A' Squadron, Sergeant Cunningham of 'C' Squadron and two troopers were killed.

On 7 May 1900, the Cavalry Division advanced through Kroonstad and Johannesburg. After engagements at Rietfontein and Doornkop, Pretoria was reached on 8 June. The *14th* fought dismounted on 11 and 12 June at Diamond Hill and despite being under continuous fire for more than 48 hours, there were few casualties. On 2 July, 59 soldiers with their horses transferred from other regiments and brought up the regimental strength to 316. Another recruit also joined on the same day. He was a baboon bought in Pretoria for the equivalent of £2.50 and was named 'Kruger' as he was thought to have some likeness to the President of the Transvaal. He remained at regimental duty until 1905.

On 8 and 9 July, the Boers attacked outposts at Deerdeport, north-east of Pretoria; despite their being isolated, the *14th* successfully drove off this onslaught. A week later a British force advanced towards the Boers' 5,000-strong laager at Bronkhorst Spruit, forcing them to retreat after several days' skirmishing. The cavalry again came under long-range fire, which could not be countered because the Horse Artillery guns were of too small a calibre. The next day 'C' Squadron, while manning outposts on

Above: 'Kruger' with the soldier who looked after him (Norwyn Photographics)

Right: Major Edward Brown, awarded the VC for conspicuous bravery at Geluk on 13 October 1900 (Norwyn Photographics)

the Olifant River, was engaged by Mausers from a distance. Regrettably the cavalry Lee-Metford carbines were unable to cope with this at such ranges. On 1 August the *14th* were given a 5-mile line of outposts to man in front of the Division at Blinkpan, south of Belfast (Bergendal). The outposts had to be held by 340 men, of whom 110 were on duty every night. Hay and forage were scarce, there was little grass and, inevitably, many of the 250 troop horses died.

On 26 August, the Regiment, the Scots Greys and Inniskilling Dragoons were in the advance-guard marching for Zwartkopjes. The following day a troop under Sergeant Dove repulsed an attack on the spur where the Regiment was in position. The march east continued over rugged and precipitous country in which it was difficult to operate effectively on horseback, but on the 31st Machadorp was reached. In September, Colonel Hamilton commanded an advance-guard consisting of the *14th* and three squadrons of Carabineers when considerable opposition was encountered at Nel's Hoek on the Komati River. Lieutenant Hill-Whitson's squadron successfully drove off the Boers while the rest of the Regiment dismounted and led their horses up the steep hill they had been ordered to occupy. The Brigade raced on for Barberton, with General French in the lead, and Captain Tottenham's squadron seized the military governor. On 15 September the town was taken and the Union Flag raised on the Court House. Several fighting reconnaissances followed, and Lieutenant the Hon. H. Grosvenor's patrol captured a party of Boers.

On 8 October, the Cavalry Division arrived at Machadorp. The *14th* regrouped into a brigade, under Colonel B. T. Mahon, 12th Lancers, with the 8th Hussars and 'M' Battery RHA. On the 12th this brigade advanced south and early next day was shelled from Geluk and very nearly surrounded. The brigade had fewer than 600 men, and the Boers were 1,000 strong. Mahon quickly withdrew the convoy, which was escorted by two reduced squadrons. He then pulled back the 8th Hussars with the remainder of the *14th* covering their withdrawal. 'A' Squadron, under Captain Charles Tottenham, came under heavy fire, and as they moved back, the 8th Hussars had two officers and several men killed. The *14th* also had two men and five horses killed.

On 13 October, Major Edward Brown showed exceptional gallantry. Under heavy fire, 400 yards from the enemy position, he saw that Sergeant Hersey's horse had been shot, so he stopped behind the last squadron as it was retiring. He helped Hersey to mount behind him and carried him to safety three-quarters of a mile away, under massive fire the while. Afterwards, and still being engaged, he held Lieutenant J. G. Browne's horse, which had become restive, enabling Browne to mount. He subsequently carried Lance-Corporal Trumpeter Leigh out of action. Major Brown was awarded the VC for conspicuous bravery in this action, the last regular officer to win the VC during Queen Victoria's reign.

The Cavalry Division then conducted a fighting withdrawal, and during a halt at Bethel, French had the *14th* paraded and congratulated them on their performance during the long and arduous campaign. In November, the *14th* encamped to the west of Pretoria, the first time they had been under canvas since leaving Bloemfontein six months previously. Three hundred remounts arrived and 212 dismounted men rejoined. New long rifles, saddlery, clothing and equipment were issued. On 21 November, Lieutenant-Colonel Gilbert Hamilton was promoted to Brigadier-General and appointed to command the 4th Cavalry Brigade, which comprised the 7th Dragoon Guards, 8th and 14th Hussars and 'O' Battery RHA. The brigade marched to Heidelberg and then Groetfontein. On 30 November the *14th* made a night march to outflank a Boer commando, under Hans Botha, in the hills north-east of Heidelberg. In December, Major Brown and 200 men cleared twelve farms and acquired a large supply of cattle, sheep and forage. Later the brigade marched to Krugersdorp, and on 19 December, two squadrons of the *14th* joined 1st Cavalry Brigade to relieve a force under Major-General Clements which was being besieged by 2,000 Boers at Hekpoort. Forty-nine of the enemy were killed, but the main body escaped to the west. The Boers also took some casualties at Vlakfontein. The brigade moved next to Hartbeestfontein and on 23 December to Stinkhoutboom 25 miles to the west. Next day, a patrol of 24 men led by Lieutenant the Hon. H. Grosvenor was surprised by 70 Boers and while managing to avoid capture, he lost 2 men and 11 horses.

Above: Lieutenant-Colonel Edmund O'Brien, who re-assumed command of the 14th in June 1901 (Courtesy Mrs Terence Gossage)

At the end of the year, Brigadier-General Gilbert Hamilton handed over command of the Brigade and was appointed administrator and commandant of Ventersdorp, west of Krugersdorp. The *14th* were divided among three brigades, prior to clearing the Southern Transvaal of Boer commandos. Operations during the early months of 1901 were not spectacular; although many Boers were killed, it was difficult to make them stand and fight. They had organised highly mobile commandos, which were to take two years to suppress. To achieve this necessary superiority farmers were evicted, brought into concentration camps and their farms burnt. Their vehicles, supplies and arms were confiscated.

In late April 1901, the *14th* were at Newcastle in the Southern Transvaal; Lieutenant-Colonel Edmund O'Brien returned from England and on 5 June resumed command. On 28 June, during continuous patrolling of the Buffalo River, Lieutenant Lace led a section which caught a party of 50 drunken Boers after they had looted a liquor store. On 17 September, 'C' Squadron was in action on the Upper Tugela. The Boers raided the local post office and hotel, taking some property belonging to local residents, but the squadron was able to drive them away, and SSM Sutherland again came into his own by shooting a Boer who had tried three times to run him through with his sword. The Boer commando was understood to have been manned by drunken Germans. On 6 October, while 'C' Squadron was employed building blockhouses, news came through that Major Brown had been promoted to Brevet Lieutenant-Colonel, that Captain Tottenham had been awarded the DSO, three privates the DCM and SSM Sutherland mentioned in dispatches.

In the meantime on 15 August, RHQ and 'B' Squadron had joined a column under Colonel Pulteney at Utrecht. This was a response to a previous reconnaissance when 500 men under Louis Botha had been encountered. After sporadic fighting, Colonel O'Brien took up positions near Nooitgedacht and posted pickets for pro-

tection. A strong outpost under Lieutenant Wright drew fire throughout the night
and, despite being sniped at all the way back, the column retired unscathed. On 2
September the column was split, and Colonel O' Brien was given command of a half-
column consisting of ' B' Squadron, the Dublin Fusiliers Mounted Infantry, a wing
of the Victoria Mounted Rifles, one gun and a pom-pom, with the task of destroying
a mill five miles ahead. Unfortunately the mill was so strongly held that it was
impossible to take it, even with heavy gun-fire. Next day the advance was resumed
with additional troops, and the Boers were shelled out of position, but the mill was
still not taken. On 8 September, the Regiment moved by rail to Newcastle. At the
same time Lieutenant Lace died as the result of an accidental discharge from his own
pistol. On 26 September, Colonel O' Brien, with 150 men, attacked a Boer position,
300 strong, at Jack's Hill. Although they were driven back, Corporal Grist was
recommended for the DCM.

On 4 January 1902 the Regiment was involved in a small action near Vrede, and
two Boers were killed. On the 21st Colonel O'Brien took a mobile column consisting
of RHQ and 'C' Squadron *14th Hussars*, one squadron 3rd Hussars and 100 men of
the Middlesex Regiment south through Konigsberg to Muller's Pass to guard the
construction of blockhouses. This duty lasted until 20 February when the *14th*, 480
strong, concentrated at Harrismith, the first time they were all together since December 1900. Brown was now second-in-command.

In 1901, the *20th Hussars*, in India and preparing for service in the Boer War, were
also starting to establish their reputation on the polo field; the Regiment won the
Indian Inter-Regimental Tournament for the first time by defeating the 15th Hussars
in the final.

In November, the Regiment left Mhow for South Africa, spent Christmas at sea
and arrived at Newcastle with 20 officers and 666 soldiers early in 1902. Both the
14th and the *20th* took part in the subsequent operations. Blockhouse lines had been
constructed along the railway between Harrismith and Kroonstad and between Frank-
fort and Heilbron to the north. In a preliminary drive against De Wet's commando,
which was operating between the blockhouses, 300 prisoners were taken, but De Wet
escaped. On 21 February the *20th* advanced south from Perdekop with two squadrons
forward. The *14th* were dismounted and dug in along the wire between the blockhouses, in positions that covered attacks from the rear as well as the front. The
trapped Boers were unable to break out, and eventually 65 were killed and 735 were
captured; 28,000 head of cattle were also taken. A casualty of the Regiment was
Captain Tottenham's borrowed troop horse, which was accidentally shot by a sentry
while Tottenham was visiting the line. His only comment was to congratulate the
soldier on his shooting.

On 15 May 1902, a two weeks' peace conference assembled at Vereeniging,
conducted by members of Kitchener's staff, who had fought in the war. Each side
respected their former enemies, and negotiations were carried out in a civilised
manner. Kitchener went out of his way to be friendly to his former opponents.

The *14th*, however, took part in the last actions of the war in the east of the
Orange Free State. They were at Lindley on 1 June when a signal was received that

peace had been declared. On the 20th they marched to Kroonstad and the *20th* went to Pretoria. Both regiments remained in their respective garrisons for a year, and enjoyed harmonious relations with the returning Boer farmers, despite their privations during the fighting. In the entire campaign the *14th* had 5 officers and 84 soldiers killed and the *20th* had 8 soldiers killed.

On 12 March 1903, the *14th* were ordered back to England. The Boers came in from the country to buy the horses; one of those sold, unhappy in its new surroundings, returned unexpectedly, jumped the wire round the camp and returned to the horse lines. Sadly, the old grey mule, which had carried the Maxim gun throughout the war, had broken down and was destroyed before the Regiment left. The *14th* embarked in the SS *Dunera* at Cape Town on 24 March for Durban where the *20th* boarded. The latter disembarked at Suez on 10 April and marched to Abbassia Barracks in Cairo to relieve the *11th Hussars*. The *14th* disembarked at

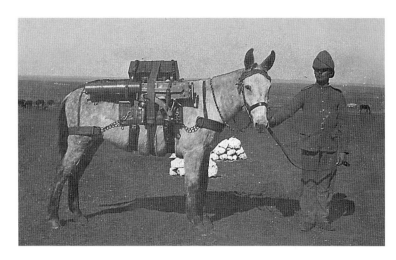

Left: The mule that carried the Maxim Gun throughout the war (Courtesy Mrs Terence Gossage)

Centre left: 20th Hussars Band at Brighton, 1906 (Steve Day; courtesy The King's Royal Hussars)

Bottom left: 20th Hussars, 1904 (Steve Day; courtesy The King's Royal Hussars)

Below: Corporal Frederick Bradley with his wife and children at Bangalore. Sadly, the boy on his mother's knee died shortly after this photograph was taken (Courtesy Douglas Hill)

Southampton on 4 May and moved to the West Cavalry Barracks at Aldershot. The march through the town was noteworthy for 'Kruger', the baboon, who walked behind the Band in some style, evidently enjoying himself.

The *20th Hussars* only remained in Egypt for a year and returned to England in November 1904. An article in the *Sussex Daily News*, dated 26 November 1904, said:

CAIRO'S LOSS, BRIGHTON'S GAIN

The people of Brighton will be glad to have such a smart regiment quartered in the town, for the 20th has ever borne that reputation. Private letters from Cairo express the greatest regret at its approaching departure from the 'Land of the Pharaohs', the loss to Cairo society will be a great gain to Brighton life, not to mention the fillip to trade, which the presence of a sporting regiment invariably gives.

In October 1904, the *14th King's Hussars* moved to Shorncliffe and in June 1905 joined the 2nd Cavalry Brigade, on its formation, which included the 7th Dragoon Guards and the *20th Hussars*. In September 1906 the *20th* relieved the *14th* at Shorncliffe, when the latter sailed from Southampton for India. The Second-in-Command was Lieutenant-Colonel Edward Browne-Synge-Hutchinson, VC, who had changed his name by deed poll from Brown two years before. The Regiment arrived at Bangalore on 29 September.

In 1906 the *20th Hussars* repeated their Indian success by winning the English Inter-Regimental Polo Championship for the first time, beating the *11th Hussars* by 6 goals to 5, and repeated this in 1907, by 6 goals to 4; but the *11th* avenged their two defeats by winning the Cup in 1909. These achievements by the *20th* were not to be repeated for seventy years. In 1908, the *20th* sailed for the Curragh after sending a draft of 72 soldiers to join the *14th* in India.

On 24 July 1909, Colonel Browne-Synge-Hutchinson, now in command of the *14th*, re-instituted the Regimental Medal (illustrated overleaf) to reward any Officer, WO, NCO or Man of the Regiment who contributed in some conspicuous manner to its military efficiency or military honour. The first recipient was SSM Dove, who had so distinguished himself in the Boer War, and the second was Sergeant Goddard, later RSM and winner of the Military Cross during the First World War. In November 1911, the *14th King's Hussars* moved from Bangalore to Mhow. The *20th Hussars* remained in Ireland until 1911 when they were posted to Colchester.

Above: The Regimental Medal, worn on the right breast on regimental occasions, was re-instituted by Colonel Edward Browne-Synge-Hutchinson, VC, in 1909, and is still awarded today (Norwyn Photographics)

Left: Trumpeter William Willis enlisted in the 20th Hussars in 1912 as a boy soldier. In 1917, he transferred to the 10th Hussars, which his son, John, commanded in 1965 (retiring as a major-general in 1981). His grandson, Hugo, is now a captain in The King's Royal Hussars (Norwyn Photographics; courtesy Major-General John Willis)

Below left: The 20th Hussars Cookhouse at the Royal Tournament before the First World War. Health & Safety at Work regulations were clearly more flexible then! (Norwyn Photographics)

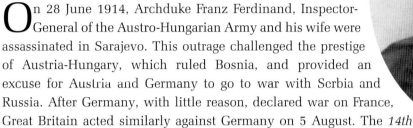

THE FIRST WORLD WAR

9

On 28 June 1914, Archduke Franz Ferdinand, Inspector-General of the Austro-Hungarian Army and his wife were assassinated in Sarajevo. This outrage challenged the prestige of Austria-Hungary, which ruled Bosnia, and provided an excuse for Austria and Germany to go to war with Serbia and Russia. After Germany, with little reason, declared war on France, Great Britain acted similarly against Germany on 5 August. The *14th King's Hussars* were still in India, and the *20th* were at Colchester in 5th Cavalry Brigade, with the Royal Scots Greys and 12th Royal Lancers.

Above right: Lieutenant-Colonel Graham Edwards led the 20th Hussars into action in France in August 1914

Below: Lieutenant Harold Soames was one of the 20th's first casualties, killed leading a reconnaissance patrol at the Battle of Mons

FRANCE 1914

On 4 August, the *20th* were ordered to mobilise. Reservists arrived, detached officers rejoined, and so many horses appeared that a remount depot had to be opened nearby. Two weeks later, the Regiment, under Lieutenant-Colonel Graham 'Pom' Edwards, left for 'an unknown destination,' and a week after that, was in action. The *20th* disembarked at Le Havre on 17 August and were warmly welcomed by the French. They then crossed into Belgium to Binche, east of Mons.

The British Army was on the left flank of the Allied armies. The 5th Cavalry Brigade was deployed on the right flank of the British Army, with the roles of reconnaissance to the front and liaison between British I Corps and French Fifth Army. The *20th* sent out patrols the first night, and the first actual contact was made on the 22nd by patrols led by Lieutenants R. M. Thompson and Joe Goodhart.

On 23 August, as the Battle of Mons started, the *20th* were in brigade reserve, south of Binche, and horses were off saddled. One of their first casualties was Lieutenant Harold Soames, killed leading a reconnaissance patrol. At 1700 the *20th* moved to Givry and came under shell-fire for the first time, which fortunately fell short. While the BEF was holding the Germans well along the line of the Mons–Condé Canal, it became exposed as the French were forced back, so it was decided to withdraw and the *20th* formed part of the rear-guard. They saddled up at 0400 on 24 August and moved back into dismounted positions along the Mons–Maubeuge road. From there, 'B' Squadron stopped a minor infantry attack before retiring farther to the south-west of Maubeuge. The withdrawal continued, and although many men were often asleep in the saddle, all were well fed. On the 28th the Brigade went into action at Moy, on the Sambre and Oise Canal, against an attack from St-Quentin. The Greys, 12th Lancers and 'J' Battery RHA charged the enemy cavalry, and Colonel Edwards led the *20th* on the left flank to divert fire away from the rest of the brigade.

On 31 August the *20th* crossed the Aisne near Soissons, and Lieutenants D'Arcy Hall and R. W. Sparrow led reconnaissance patrols to establish whether the enemy had crossed. Hall reported that Germans held the bridge at Ambleny, with a squadron to the south. As he extricated his patrol,

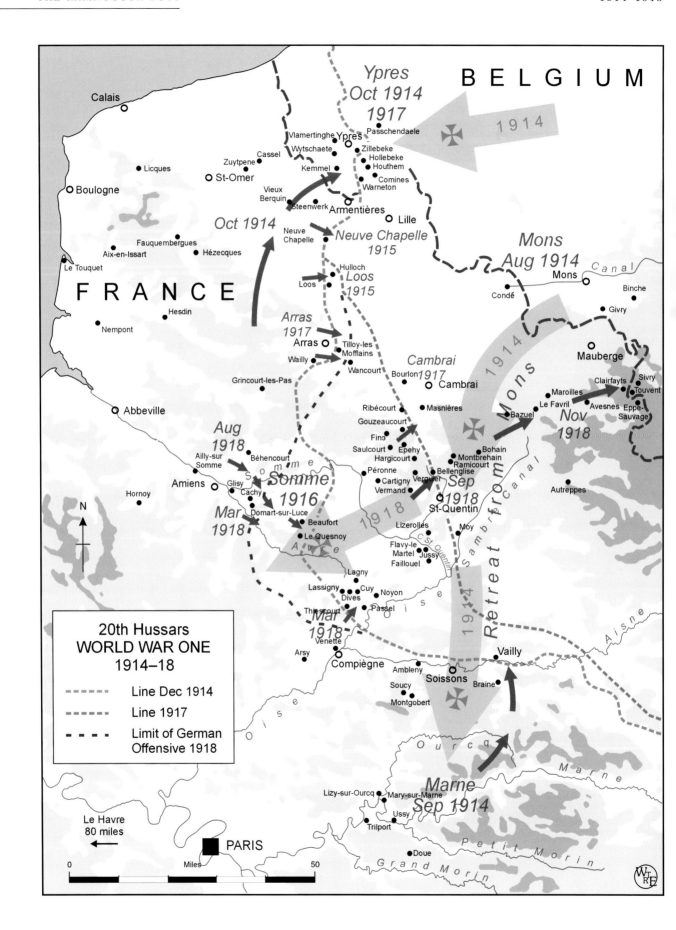

BELGIUM

Ypres
Oct 1914
1917

Passchendaele

Calais

Vlamertinghe • Ypres
Wytschaete
Zillebeke
Hollebeke
Houthem
Kemmel
Comines
Warneton

Licques

Zuytpene • Cassel

St-Omer

Vieux Berquin
Steenwerk • Armentières

Lille

Boulogne

Oct 1914

Neuve Chapelle

Neuve Chapelle
1915

Mons
Aug 1914

Canal

Mons

Condé

Binche

Givry

Fauquembergues
Aix-en-Issart • Hézecques

Le Touquet

F R A N C E

Hulloch
Loos

Loos
1915

Hesdin

Nempont

Arras
1917

Arras
Tilloy-les-Mofflains
Wailly
Wancourt

Grincourt-les-Pas

Cambrai
1917

Bourlon

Cambrai

Masnières

Mauberge

Clairfayts
Sivry
Touvent
Le Favril
Avesnes
Eppe-Sauvage
Maroilles
Bazuel

Mons

Nov
1918

Abbeville

Ribécourt
Gouzeaucourt

Aug
1918

Ailly-sur-Somme

Béhencourt

Somme

Fins
Saulcourt • Epehy
Hargicourt
Péronne
Cartigny
Vermand

Bohain
Montbrehain
Ramicourt
Bellenglise
Vermand
Verguier

Autreppes

Somme
1916

Amiens

Glisy
Cachy
Domart-sur-Luce

Sep
1918

St-Quentin

1918

Retreat from

Hornoy

N

Mar
1918

Beaufort
Le Quesnoy

Avre

Lizerolles
Moy

Flavy-le-Martel
Jussy
Faillouel

Lagny

Lassigny • Cuy • Noyon
Dives
Passel
Thiescourt

Mar
1918

Venette

Arsy

Compiègne

Ambleny

Soucy
Montgobert

Soissons • Braine

Vailly

Aisne

Sambre from Canal

1914

Oise

Ourcq

Marne

20th Hussars
WORLD WAR ONE
1914–18

- - - - -   Line Dec 1914
- - - - -   Line 1917
- - - - -   Limit of German
               Offensive 1918

Marne
Sep 1914

Lizy-sur-Ourcq • Mary-sur-Marne
Ussy
Trilport

Le Havre
80 miles

PARIS

Miles

0   50

Doue

Petit Morin

Grand Morin

they came under attack from a position 400 yards away. Hall's rear point, Private Hayhurst, drew his sword and charged single-handed, completely disconcerting the enemy, who retreated to Soucy at the gallop. This action illustrates the commitment and morale of the *20th* in 1914; it was sad that Hayhurst was killed, as a lance-corporal, two years later. Sparrow's patrol had similar success, when a German troop approached Sergeant Goodwin's section, which opened fire, and the enemy beat another hasty retreat.

As the fighting withdrawal continued, cunning bursts of fire deceived the Germans into thinking the opposition was greater than it was. In 'A' Squadron, Sergeant Cook was wounded, but when told that his mare, on which he had won the Sergeants' Light-Weight Point-to-Point, was to be sent to another regiment, he discharged himself from an ambulance, recovered his horse and rejoined his squadron.

By 2 September the Regiment had withdrawn to Trilport, 'C' Squadron holding the bridges at Mary-sur-Marne and Lizy-sur-Ourcq. Sparrow's troop fired on enemy patrols, but a strong mounted force counter-attacked, and Corporal Garness was killed, which prompted Major Mangles to withdraw 'C' Squadron. This delaying action allowed the brigade safely to pull back over the Marne at Ussy. 'B' Squadron went forward to cover the final retirement, but had several men killed, including Captain Simon Christy. The last man to cross the bridge, before it was blown, was Colonel 'Pom' Edwards.

Above: Captain Simon Christy, killed covering the brigade's with-drawal over the river Marne

Brigade HQ and RHQ were set up at Doué. Despite orders to withhold fire, Lieutenant Goodhart's troop missed a German motor-cyclist at 50 yards, reinforcing 'C' Squadron's ignominious reputation for marksmanship, acquired on the ranges at Lydd. The Germans were then seen to be de-bussing and deploying for an attack so the Regiment therefore took up positions at Doué. 'A' and 'B' Squadrons fought a number of rear-guard actions until they reached a bivouac area south of Rozay-en-Brie. So ended the retreat from Mons, about which General von Moltke, wrote in his memoirs: 'That the complete defeat of France in our first advance did not come off, was due to the rapid assistance brought to her by England.'

On 6 September, the Allied counter-offensive, known as the Battle of the Marne, began. The *20th* led the 5th Cavalry Brigade north. The first two days were uneventful apart from Corporal Goring killing two retreating Uhlans and capturing their lances. Despite coming under some light artillery fire, the regiment crossed the Marne on the 9th. The CinC rode round the brigade in the afternoon and said how well everyone had done during the retreat. The pursuit continued on the 10th with 'B' Squadron in the lead, but heavy fighting on both flanks prevented an effective follow-up. The Regiment then moved into billets at Braine. At the same time, 3rd and 5th Cavalry Brigades were formed into the 2nd Cavalry Division under General Gough.

On 14 September the *20th* crossed the Aisne at Vailly by a pontoon bridge and came under artillery fire. The colonel dismounted the Regiment, and horses were led over in single file into the town. On arrival the infantry forward positions were so heavily shelled that a return was necessary, taking casualties.

Trench warfare had now started along the Aisne. Sir John French re-deployed the British Army on the left of the Allied line, with a view to turning the German flank and easing re-supply from the Channel ports. The 2nd Cavalry Division reached Amiens on 7 October, and on the 12th 'A' Squadron led the brigade advance-guard east. 'C' Squadron, with the Greys, made a dismounted attack on Mont-des-Cats, a knoll south-west of Ypres. Next day the *20th* advanced to Comines, over the Belgian frontier. Two troops from 'C' Squadron fought the Germans through the villages of Hollebeke and Houthem, and 'A' and 'B' Squadrons dismounted driving the enemy back along the line of the Kortekeer Beck.

On 20 October the *20th* dug a defensive position east of the Oosttaverne–Warneton road; no mean task, because picks and shovels had been left behind during the pursuit over the Marne. Mess tins and cutlery were used until the local inhabitants could be persuaded to part with their spades. As the German positions were only 800 yards away, solid trenches had to be constructed. Most were surprised that the cavalry regiment should dig itself in without its horses, which were kept behind the line. Over the next ten days of assaults and shelling, the brigade was forced to withdraw when the Germans occupied Wytschaete. The 12th Lancers, supported, by 'B' Squadron under Captain Arthur Little, successfully counter-attacked, but the enemy then put down so effective a bombardment that a move back was again necessary. Lieutenant McConnel, with the machine-gun section, covered this withdrawal and was the last to leave; Little and McConnel were both awarded the DSO. On 19 November, the *20th* took over trenches at Kemmel from French Chasseurs Alpins, who were surprised that the *20th* had so many officers there, including the squadron leader. When in French hands, the position was commanded by a sergeant, who said that he did not think that it was smart enough for a major. The Regiment remained there for two days and had six casualties from heavy shelling.

After the First Battle of Ypres, the *20th* were relieved by the 5th Dragoon Guards, mounted their horses and moved to billets at Steenwerk. They had been fortunate in not being heavily attacked so far, and casualties had been relatively light. On 2 December 1914 the King inspected the Regiment, and 72-hour leave passes were granted so that all ranks might go back to England.

MESOPOTAMIA 1915

While the *20th Hussars* were in France, the *14th* moved to Meerut in November 1914, and were disappointed not to leave India with the reinforcements for the Western Front. It has been suggested that the Prussian Eagle badge did not help the *14th*'s case for fighting the Germans. At an Officers' Mess meeting in May 1915, it was decided to stop wearing the 'Hawk' cap badge, in view of its German connections, and to adopt the alternative 'Royal Crest within the Garter', which decision was approved by the Army Council.

The *14th* received the long-awaited order to mobilise on 27 October 1915, but not for France, there being sufficient cavalry on the Western Front. The *14th* were bound for Mesopotamia, an area in the Middle East, between the Euphrates and Tigris, and now part of Iraq. The previous year, Turkey had joined Germany in the Central Powers, and was threatening the Persian oil-fields. The 6th Indian Division, under Major-General Charles Townshend, was sent, but after successes and reverses, another British cavalry regiment was required to assist in the permanent occupation of Baghdad. On 14 November, the *14th King's Hussars* arrived at Basra.

Above: Sergeant Simes, awarded the DCM for gallantry during a counter-attack at Zillebeke on 15 January 1915 (Norwyn Photographics; courtesy Douglas Hill)

FRANCE 1915

On 15 January, the *20th* withdrew to Fauquemberges, east of Boulogne. After infantry training, they joined 'B' Dismounted Brigade in 2nd Cavalry Division and took over trenches at Zillebeke east of Ypres. Life was quiet until 21 February when the 16th Lancers lost a trench with heavy casualties. 'C' Squadron sent reinforcements to help in an unsuccessful counter-attack, having several officers and men killed and wounded; Sergeant Simes was awarded the DCM for gallantry during the attack. On the 23rd the Regiment was relieved, returned to Fauquemberges, then on 9 March, took part in an attack on Neuve Chapelle and subsequent pursuit.

On 26 April, the Regiment dismounted once more and occupied reserve trenches at Potijze east of Ypres. While there, shelling killed several men and a gas attack resulted in basic respirators being issued. On 14 May the *20th* took over trenches at Vlamertinghe from the 3rd Dragoon Guards who, despite losing 80 men including their Commanding Officer, had fought most effectively. The Regiment improved the badly damaged trenches, helped by an infantry working-party. On the 24th, after another gas attack, the 5th Cavalry Brigade went into divisional reserve, the Regiment moving to comfortable billets at Zuytpeene, for four months, and the horses were happily turned out in the open.

On 6 August, the *20th* moved to Wittes, south-east of St-Omer, and managed to play polo, with a small football, as the ground was rough. While there, squadron horses were re-organised by colours: 'A' was supposed to have bays, 'B' blacks and browns, and 'C' chestnuts. This was not an entirely harmonious exercise, because their riders were loath to lose good mounts to other squadrons because of their colour.

On 21 September, the *20th* marched south for the Battle of Loos during which Sergeant George Withers showed conspicuous gallantry in stationing the night listening-

Below: Digging support trenches in April/May 1915 (Norwyn Photographics)

Below right: Watering the horses at Wittes, south-east of St-Omer (Norwyn Photographics)

posts and the advanced posts by day, for which he was awarded the DCM. On 29 September the *20th* were withdrawn, Colonel 'Pom' Edwards was given command of an infantry brigade, and was succeeded by Major George Cook. On 16 November, the Regiment moved into winter quarters at Fauquemberges, and a period of intensive infantry training followed.

MESOPOTAMIA 1915

After landing at Basra, the *14th King's Hussars* transferred to river steamers, sailed up the Tigris for Kut-al-Amara and were concentrated there by 23 November 1915. The day before, Townshend had defeated the Turks at Ctesiphon, capturing 1,300 prisoners and eight guns, but losing one third of his forces. However, the Turks quickly brought up reinforcements, and the British were forced to withdraw.

On 25 November, the Regiment, under the command of Major Robert Hewitt, was ordered to march to Aziziyeh with two companies of the Royal West Kents; this took three days because of deep mud. The *14th* were welcomed by General Townshend who, although a controversial figure, had been a good friend to the Regiment in Bangalore. The first action was at El Kutunie, where 'A' Squadron, under Lieutenant Jack Miller, charged a party of enemy with great effect, and a troop under Lieutenant Dick Woodhouse pursued Turks fleeing towards the Tigris. Somewhat exaggerated reports of these successes went round the theatre, but they did prove that the *14th* meant business. In a dispatch, General Townshend said: 'The advent of the *14th Hussars* (British) has put new spirit and dash into the Indian Cavalry.'

As the withdrawal continued, on 1 December, a concentration of Turkish troops attempted to surround the division. The *14th* dismounted, and supported by the Machine-Gun Section under Lieutenant 'Darky' Pope, put down effective fire against an enemy line. This stopped the Turks and allowed Townshend to continue the withdrawal; although under heavy shell-fire the *14th* trotted back in good order, living up to their reputation as the best-drilled regiment in India. However as a long enemy column was attempting to turn the right flank, the *14th* were ordered to attack. The Regiment drew swords and charged, and the enemy dispersed in all directions. This action, the Battle of Umm-al-Tabal, cost the Turks 1,500 casualties. The Regiment lost five men killed.

The British withdrawal, during which General Townshend lost 4,567 men, ended on 3 December when the Division reached Kut-al-Amara, which Townshend unwisely decided to hold, though happily without the 6th Cavalry Brigade. The Regiment, less a guard of sixteen men with the heavy baggage, marched downstream to Ali-al-Gharbi, and after a skirmish with 1,200 Arab horsemen, arrived on 8 December. The siege of Kut, surrounded by four Turkish divisions under Nur-ed-Din, began.

Left: Sergeant George Withers, awarded the DCM for conspicuous gallantry at the battle of Loos (Courtesy Douglas Hill)

Right, top to bottom: Episodes in Mesopotamia as depicted by the sketches of Private Moses Baggott – Arrival of the 14th in a swampy bivouac area at Kut-al-Amara on 25 November 1915 – The 14th drive back two regiments of Turkish cavalry at the battle of Umm-al-Tabal on 1 December 1915 – Withdrawal of the cavalry brigade from Kut-al-Amara on 6 December 1915 – After an infantry attack on 21 January 1916, the order to pursue was awaited, but administrative problems made this impossible. Private Baggott served throughout the war in Mesopotamia, and his sketchbook of some fifty drawings is now on display in the museum at Preston (Norwyn Photographics)

1916

The first attempt at relief took place after the arrival of two more Indian Divisions. An advance to Sheikh Saad, upstream started on 3 January with the *14th* leading the 6th Cavalry Brigade on the left flank. During heavy fighting over three days, SSM Wright galloped up to a Turkish trench and fired his pistol to create a diversion. This caused the Turks to withdraw, and Wright was awarded the DCM. Administrative problems, to say nothing of 4,000 casualties, prevented any pursuit.

On 15 February Brigadier-General Robert Stephen, who had commanded the *14th* in India, took over command of the 6th Cavalry Brigade. The last attempt to relieve Kut was made on 5 April, with the cavalry brigade covering the open flank. The three divisions involved took very heavy casualties, but to no avail. On 29 April 1916, Townshend surrendered. A total of 13,259 officers, soldiers and non-combatants went into a captivity which few survived. Not so Townshend who spent his captivity in comfort. The decision to hold Kut had little justification, apart from vanity, and it cost the British more than 40,000 casualties. Its loss was the worst disaster suffered by the British army between Yorktown in 1781 and Singapore in 1942.* Townshend was however still awarded a knighthood.

FRANCE 1916

On 3 January the *20th Hussars* were re-organised as a company in the 5th Dismounted Battalion, initially under Lieutenant-Colonel Collins of the Greys. On the 7th Captain John Darling took over the company which rotated between huts west of Vermelles, support trenches and front-line trenches. This ground had

*The Marquess of Anglesea. *A History of the British Cavalry 1816–1919*

been occupied during the Battle of Loos, and included its 'chateau', a red brick villa. Successful tactics were sniping, careful siting of machine-guns, nightly reconnaissance patrols and bombing raids by parties with Mills grenades. On 13 February, while Major Arthur Little was commanding the company, the Germans made bombing attacks, and the *20th* retaliated with two attacks under Lieutenants Hatton and Jeffrey; the latter and seven men were killed. On 15 February, the *20th* company was relieved and moved back to Fauquemberges.

In March, RSM Austin was commissioned and joined 'A' Squadron, and SSM Rabjohn became RSM. In April, the Regiment moved to Licques east of Boulogne. On 7 June, the 5th Dismounted Battalion, now under Lieutenant-Colonel George Cook, hastily moved in buses to Zillebeke in support of the Canadians who had had heavy losses. A successful counter-attack by the Canadian Corps on

18 June allowed the Regiment to become part of Second Army mobile reserve, based at Verte Rue in the Forêt de Nieppe. On 6 September the *20th* left Second Army for the Somme offensive. Patrolling took place, and mounted training, but the weather prevented further use of cavalry before winter, and on 8 November, the *20th* withdrew to winter quarters near Hesdin.

MESOPOTAMIA 1916

After the fall of Kut in April, the *14th* camped at Gomorrah on the south bank of the Tigris four miles west of Ali-al-Gharbi. Wet weather, flies and poor conditions took their toll, many suffered fever, jaundice or dysentery, and one man died of cholera. Lieutenant-Colonel Thomas Hill-Whitson and seventeen men were invalided home and Major Robert Hewitt resumed command. The Army of the Tigris was ordered to contain the Turks at Kut and prevent them from sending troops to face the Russian advance through Persia. For a month, two squadrons of the *14th* rode out on daily reconnaissance patrols until 19 May when they marched to positions, partially vacated by the Turks, at Es Sinn on the south bank of the Tigris.

At 0330 on 21 May, the cavalry brigade was ordered to secure a Turkish pontoon bridge across the Shatt-al-Hai. 'B' Squadron led the brigade, and at first light came under enemy fire. Lieutenant Deakin's troop in 'D' Squadron, sent forward to establish the position of the bridge, dismounted and opened fire. Hewitt then brought the Regiment into action, but could only muster 150 rifles, and being severely outnumbered, the brigadier ordered them to withdraw. Captain Mewburn and Lieutenant Deakin were both killed during the retirement. When the hot weather began, the Regiment was withdrawn to a camp on the south bank of the Tigris, known as Arab Village, where it remained until the end of the year.

On 10 December, an advance on the Shatt-al-Hai began. The offensive opened with a heavy artillery barrage against the enemy positions at Sanna-i-Yat and the Cavalry Division crossed the river at Basrugieh on the 13th. This move surprised the Turks, and opposition was light until the force reached Shumran, when it came under effective rifle fire, and shelling from a gun-boat on the Tigris. The divisional commander hesitated to rush the bridge until he had information about the enemy. Captain T. R. Bruce with 'B' Squadron galloped up under heavy fire to within 700 yards of the bridge, located the Turkish positions and withdrew. Operations were then curtailed until January 1917 because of the weather and mud.

FRANCE 1917

In January the *20th Hussars* were in billets at Nempont near the coast where they practised 'gap' training, which involved passing through a break in the enemy line, made by the infantry. The horses were less than fit because there had been a shortage of oats throughout the winter. On 5 April they moved to Grincourt-lès-Pas to await the coming offensive. The weather was very wet and spirits was not particularly high. On 9 April, the march continued to 'Telegraph Hill', a feature just west of Tilloy-les-Mofflains, captured by the infantry that morning; the 2nd Cavalry Division was concentrated there by 1615. As the Regiment was moving back to Wailly at 2030, many horses stumbled into shell-holes, never to get out again. On 10 April, 5th Cavalry Brigade galloped to an enemy position near Wancourt, and a snowstorm fortunately prevented enemy observers directing fire. While wire eventually halted the Regiment, the Germans evacuated their positions, but the *20th* held firm during what turned out to be the most uncomfortable night of the war for both men and horses. The troops were admirably steady, and apart from shelling, there was no enemy counter-attack. At 1300 the 5th Cavalry Brigade withdrew to Wailly. During the Battle of Arras, the *20th* lost one man killed, two officers and five men wounded and 37 horses killed. Since the Brigade lost 477 horses, the Regiment had got off lightly.

During the summer the *20th* had periods in the trenches and carried out both mounted and dismounted training. The extremely costly Battle of Passchendaele was fought from August to November, but without cavalry, and on 20 October the *20th* were in winter quarters at Wailly. They were not destined to stay there long because the Battle of Cambrai was looming.

MESOPOTAMIA 1917

Early in the year, preparations for an advance on Baghdad were begun. On 18 January the cavalry division raided Kut-al-Hai, and the *14th* made a dismounted attack along the Massag Canal. On 24 February, the Turks were in full retreat and the division started to pursue across the Tigris at Shumran. As the bridge was damaged, the crossing took several hours, and the enemy could not be routed. On the 25th the Army Commander, Lieutenant-General Sir Frederick Maude, gave orders for the cavalry to reach Bughaila by nightfall and for the Turkish commander, Imam Mahdi, to be captured. The Regiment made a dismounted attack against the enemy's rear-guard, again jeopardising an effective pursuit. On the 26th, the cavalry division moved round the enemy left flank, supported by the fire of three gun-boats, and struck at Bughaila. The Turks abandoned the town and the follow-up continued. Three miles from Aziziyeh, 6th Cavalry Brigade came under heavy shelling, so the *14th* rode round to find the enemy flank. Subsequent patrols led by Captain Bridges and Lieutenant Whadcoat located the Turkish field guns and reported an apparent break down in discipline. Eight guns were later taken by Lieutenant Macintyre's troop, and Major-General Crocker presented two of the gun plates to the Regiment.

On 1 March Aziziyeh was found to be free of enemy, and the advance on Baghdad began. Captain A. G. L. Astley led 'D' Squadron in a dismounted attack against positions in the dry river-beds, but heavy Turkish fire killed Astley and Corporal Howarth; this delayed the squadron, so Brigadier-General Holland-Pryor ordered the *14th* to withdraw. However this attack, and a mounted charge made by the 13th

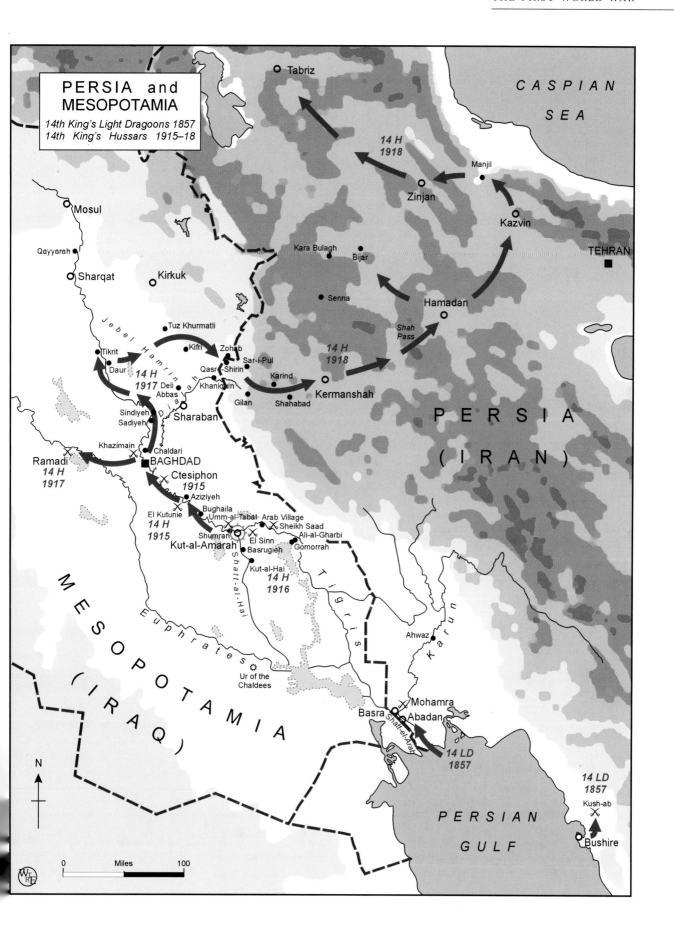

PERSIA and MESOPOTAMIA
14th King's Light Dragoons 1857
14th King's Hussars 1915–18

CASPIAN
SEA

Tabriz

Mosul

Qayyarah

Sharqat

Kirkuk

Kara Bulagh

Bijar

Senna

Tuz Khurmatli

Kifri

Zohab

Sar-i-Pul

Tikrit

Daur

*14 H
1917*

Qasr-i-Shirin

Karind

Deli
Abbas

Khaniqin

Gilan

Shahabad

Kermanshah

*Shah
Pass*

*14 H
1918*

Hamadan

*14 H
1918*

Zinjan

Manjil

Kazvin

TEHRAN

Sindiyeh
Sadiyeh

Sharaban

Khazimain

Chaldari

BAGHDAD

Ramadi
*14 H
1917*

*Ctesiphon
1915*

Aziziyeh

El Kutunie
*14 H
1915*

Bughaila

Umm-al-Tabal

Arab Village

Sheikh Saad

Shumran

El Sinn

Basrugieh

Ali-al-Gharbi

Gomorrah

Kut-al-Amarah

Kut-al-Hai
*14 H
1916*

PERSIA

(IRAN)

MESOPOTAMIA

(IRAQ)

Euphrates

Ur of the
Chaldees

Tigris

Ahwaz

Karun

Mohamra

Basra

Abadan

*14 LD
1857*

N

PERSIAN

GULF

*14 LD
1857*

Kush-ab

Bushire

0   Miles   100

ENTRY OF THE GLADIATORS INTO BAGHDAD. MAR. 11. 1917

Hussars, forced the Turks to evacuate the position. On the 6 March, the brigade passed through Ctesiphon, and a long-range patrol, led by Lieutenant Moule, obtained information about the enemy dispositions and took 43 prisoners. Baghdad was captured on 10 March, and next day Lieutenant-Colonel Robert Hewitt led a party of the *14th Hussars* into Khazimain, to the west, received its surrender, and returned with 100 prisoners, some being British, whom the Turks had released.

On 27 March, the Turks were in strength around Deli Abbas, north-east of Baghdad. 'B' and 'C' Squadrons were in dismounted positions on the Deli Abbas road.

Right: *Deli Abbas, March 1917 – the rescue of Lieutenant Sam Hamer, as sketched by Private Baggott. During the withdrawal from Deli Abbas, Lieutenant Sam Hamer was seriously wounded and was galloped out of action by Sergeant-Farrier Hayward. Hamer's son, Peter, was to command the 11th Hussars in Germany during the Cold War (Norwyn Photographics)*

In a fierce action, in which the 21st and 22nd Cavalry and 'S' Battery RHA took part, both squadrons came under heavy fire, mounted their horses, galloped to the rear and continued the fight, supported by 'A' and 'B' Squadrons. On 12 April the Turks began to withdraw.

On 23 April the Regiment was recalled to Baghdad to join a punitive expedition against certain Arab villages on the Euphrates to avenge the murder of a British officer. The column included *2nd/6th Gurkha Rifles*, the first time the two regiments had served together. General Holland-Pryor was reluctant to lose the *14th*, saying, generously that they were the best regiment he had ever seen. However the expedition was to be short-lived, and he was to see them again at Chaldari on 12 May. The exceptionally hot weather then began, and summer training started.

On the Euphrates, the Turks had a 1,000-strong detachment at Ramadi. The 7th Infantry Brigade was sent in the extreme heat to deal with it, but was beaten off and retired. The enemy then reinforced the town, and by September had 120 cavalry, 3,500 infantry, 12 guns and about 1,000 Arab irregulars there. General Maude therefore sent in a substantial formation, which included the 6th Cavalry Brigade. The *14th* left Chaldari on 18 September, under Lieutenant-Colonel Robert Hewitt. The squadron leaders were Captains John Woodhouse, Ambler, Bridges and Fetherstonhaugh. They reached an assembly area at Madhi, north of the river, on 28 September. After a successful infantry attack, which included *2nd/6th Gurkhas*, the 6th Cavalry Brigade crossed the river to the road west of Ramadi without being observed. Fifty horsemen were pursued back into the town, and some casualties were received from the fire from Turkish gunboats. The *14th* then dismounted and took up blocking positions on the road, with a troop on the bank of the river. The

Below: *Sketch map of the Battle of Ramadi, 29 September 1917 (Sketch by Captain Jack Miller)*

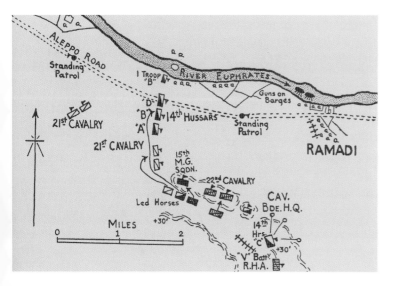

22nd Cavalry was on their right and the 21st was watching the rear. Standing patrols were sent out east towards Ramadi under Lieutenant Moule, and west towards Hit under Lieutenant Gillanders.

At 1800 the Regiment was ordered to stop the enemy from breaking out along the Aleppo road. At 0100 on 29 September, Moule reported 40 enemy cavalry and 400 infantry moving west along the river. At 0245 the Colonel gave the order to open fire, and every rifle in the line and the ten Hotchkiss light machine-guns did so in a volley. Although the enemy made some response, the initial salvo by the *14th* decided the outcome. Unfortunately a blazing barge on the river distorted the troops' night vision and the moon, sinking behind the brigade, silhouetted men and animals, allowing Turkish riflemen to cause many casualties. Lieutenant Meade, Sergeant McWilliams and Corporal Foulstone were killed, and a number of others wounded. At about 0400, Colonel Hewitt, in the centre of the line, was shot; he died at Falluha hospital two days later. 'C' Squadron Leader, Captain Edgar Bridges, assumed command of the Regiment.

That evening, the 21st Cavalry pursued the Turks upstream with the *14th* in reserve. On 30 September, the garrison at Ramadi surrendered, 3,455 prisoners were taken, thirteen guns, a large quantity of arms, ammunition and supplies were also captured. The 14th lost two officers and nine men killed, one officer and fifteen men wounded. Lieutenant Moule was awarded the Military Cross for his patrol work, and the Regiment was specially mentioned in the Divisional Commander's report. After Colonel Robert Hewitt's funeral, the *14th* returned to Chaldari on 6 October, and were congratulated by the Army Commander.

Above: Posthumous painting by A. E. Cooper of Lieutenant-Colonel Robert Hewitt, killed commanding the Regiment at Ramadi (Steve Day; courtesy The King's Royal Hussars)

Following Ramadi, much of the fight appeared to have left the Turks, and it was decided to clear them from the left bank of the river Dialah. On 23 October, the division left for Sadiyeh, north of Baghdad, and moved farther north along the Tigris over four consecutive night marches towards Daur, which 28th Infantry Brigade attacked, and the enemy retired to Tikrit. Air reconnaissance reported a force of 4,000 marching downstream. The 6th Cavalry Brigade was ordered to deal with it and moved into positions along a ridge facing north. The *14th* dug in with two squadrons forward and two 600 yards back. Disappointingly, the Turks went elsewhere, and the 13th Hussars in 7th Cavalry Brigade saw most of the action. However, the Turks had already evacuated Tikrit so the brigade returned to Sadiyeh.

On 18 November, General Maude died of cholera and at his memorial service Trumpet-Major Sandy of the *14th Hussars* sounded the 'Last Post'. On 30 November, the Regiment moved across the Tigris to Sindiyeh and took part in operations on the Jebel Hamrin. Patrols led by Lieutenants Dick Woodhouse and P. G. Cropper gained useful information, but unexpected shelling killed Sergeant Laggett of 'C' Squadron and wounded two men. On 6 December, the *14th* left their forward positions, and spent Christmas at Sadiyeh.

FRANCE 1917

The 5th Cavalry Brigade moved from its winter quarters to a hutted camp on the old
Somme battlefield. The *20th* now included a 'dismounted element' of officers and
men, which gave it more flexibility to operate in either the infantry or mounted role.
The brigade reached its assembly area at Saulcourt at 0620 on 20 November, which
was 'H' Hour for the Battle of Cambrai. The attack by 400 tanks of the Royal Tank
Corps, advancing at 2mph, was made without a preliminary bombardment, and was
followed up by six infantry divisions with two in reserve, over a six-mile front. This
achieved complete surprise and initially was a success, but next day, after patrols had
been sent out, a German counter-attack prevented further mounted action, and 5th
Cavalry Brigade was withdrawn.

On 25 November, the Regiment marched to Ribécourt, in anticipation of a
mounted exploitation which did not come off. The brigade therefore raised the '5th
Dismounted Battalion', under Lieutenant-Colonel Collins of the Greys. The *20th*
found a company of five officers and 218 men under Captain Silvertop, and horses
were sent back to a camp. The *20th* company came under artillery fire; the Medical
Officer and nine men were wounded. On the 27th the battalion moved to a small
re-entrant in Bourlon Wood. That night Captain Silvertop and Lieutenant C. N. S.
('Romulus') Woolf were killed, and Lieutenant P. S. ('Remus') Woolf was wounded, as
the result of shelling, and on 29 November, the 5th Battalion was relieved.

On the 30th the *20th* were ordered to seize high ground south-west of Gouzeaucourt and block the enemy breakthrough south of Masnières. Colonel Cook ordered
the *20th* to saddle up, and moved off quickly from Fins, where they had been having
baths. As the line of trenches was thinly held, and the Germans were only 300 yards
ahead, the Regiment reinforced the trenches before advancing further. The *20th* then
moved forward some 1,000 yards, dispatching opposition en route. On reaching the
objective, further advance was impossible because of extremely heavy enfilade fire
from the north. The Regiment remained in position all night, supported by a
squadron of the Greys. A gap on the left flank having opened, Major Little gathered
the remaining soldiers of three infantry companies who had lost their officers, and
closed it. For his performance that day, he was awarded a bar to his DSO.

The *20th* were relieved on 1 December and, justifiably, felt satisfied with their
part in the recapture of Gouzeaucourt. Over the next few days, the 5th Cavalry
Brigade was regularly stood-to ready to act mounted or dismounted. On the 6th the
Regiment marched to Cartigny and from there to Glisy, out of the battle area. On 20
December, the dismounted company, under Captain Sandford, took over trenches
from the Royal West Kents, near Péronne. The company stayed either in the front line
or in support until 29 January 1918, when it rejoined the Regiment at Hornoy.

PERSIA 1918

Lieutenant-Colonel Edgar Bridges received secret instructions to lead a small column
for duty in Persia. The column, which included 'S' Battery RHA, consisted of 34 officers, 651 soldiers, 885 horses and two guns. They set off on 13 January and arrived
at Qasr-i-Shirin, six days later. Known as 'Bridges' Column', it was to link up with a
White Russian (non-revolutionary) force of 600 Cossacks under General Bischarkov,
pending the arrival of Major-General L. C. Dunsterville, the Head of the British Military

Mission. The task of 'Dunsterforce' was to deny Persia to the Turks by re-organising those local forces abandoned by the Russian Revolutionary Government. This would involve the Regiment being extended over 500 miles between Kermanshah and the Caspian Sea.

On 23 January 'C' Squadron, under Captain 'Darky' Pope, carried out a reconnaissance of the range of hills guarding Qasr-i-Shirin from the west. A newly joined subaltern, Lieutenant Graham Paul, caricatured this somewhat scurrilously. In February. 'A' and 'B' Squadrons, under Major John Woodhouse, conducted reconnaissances throughout the area of responsibility, including protection of the telephone line running to Sar-i-Pul. On 18 February, General Bischarkov with his fine Cossacks encamped with their strong ponies alongside the Regiment en route for Hamadan.

In early March 'B' Squadron under Captain M. J. Ambler, accompanied by a political officer and 100 Persian Irregulars, carried out a punitive expedition against the Kalkhur Tribe encamped to the south. The squadron dismounted, fired at the tribesmen, killing the headman, and captured 600 cattle and

sheep. Ambler was congratulated by the GOC. During the next few days further forays caused the Column to become widely dispersed. Only 'C' Squadron remained at Qasr-i-Shirin, but it moved up to Hamadan on 11 April to reinforce Dunsterville's mission. On arrival, the horses were picketed out in a fruit garden and the men were housed in a carpet factory. On 25 April 'A' Squadron, under Major John Woodhouse, marched to the western slopes of Kuh-i-Harri, north-east of Zohab, and fired at the tribesmen on a ridge. The friendly Kuhlor tribesmen, supporting 'A' Squadron, followed up and killed the Sinjabi tribesmen, breaking their power in the area.

On 28 April 'D' Squadron, under Captain Fetherstonhaugh, supporting an infantry brigade, advanced on Kifri, north-west of Qasr-i-Shirin, and captured 70 prisoners. The 6th Cavalry Brigade charged the enemy flank at Tuz Khurmatli, and, on 7 May, Kirkuk was seized, the Turks losing 200 dead and 500 taken prisoner.

On 1 June the *14th* were dispersed over 400 miles between the rail-head at Ruz in the west and Kazvin in the east where 'C' Squadron, under Captain 'Darky' Pope, was based. On 2 June, 'A' Squadron was ordered to Kermanshah to provide a full mounted escort for the British Consul. RHQ, 'B' and 'D' Squadrons were ordered to Hamadan and

Left: *A cartoon, by Lieutenant Graham Paul, of Captain 'Darky' Pope pretending he is General Allenby* (Courtesy Edward Paul)

Left: *A cartoon, by Lieutenant Graham Paul, of Captain 'Darky' Pope pretending he is General Allenby* (Courtesy Edward Paul)

arrived there on 5 July. News was received that Major Woodhouse had been awarded the DSO and RSM Goddard, the MC. On 8 July 'D' Squadron under Lieutenant Whidborne was ordered to Bijar, followed a week later by the rest of 'Bridges' Column'.

On 16 August 'C' Squadron marched through the mountains from Manjil to Zinjan, to support a detachment operating against the Turks, under a Colonel Matthews. It arrived on the 20th in a fairly exhausted condition. Forced marches were made each day to a camp south-east of Tabriz, where companies from the Hampshires and Gurkhas joined. On 5/6 September, the Turks attacked, but the Column counter-attacked on both flanks. During the next six weeks 'C' Squadron was engaged in a fighting withdrawal to Kazvin which it reached on 31 October, to be joined five days later by 'B' Squadron.

Meanwhile 'D' Squadron, supported by armoured cars, was in action against some 500 Turks at Saln Kaleh. In a confused situation, the three troops had to fight, reorganise the Jelu levies and cope with many refugees. Twelve men, under Sergeant Hallard, successfully rescued a Dunsterforce party which had been surrounded by Turkish cavalry. Hallard was awarded the DCM.

Left: *The road from Kazvin to Menjil, in north-west Persia, where the 14th were widely dispersed in 1918, as sketched by Private Baggott* (Norwyn Photographics)

In September, after Dunsterville had evacuated the port of Baku, there was concern that the Turks would sense British weakness in the area. 'C' Squadron was reckoned to be vulnerable, but these fears were allayed after Major-General W. M. Thompson was placed in command of all troops in North Persia. Bridges' Column, now at Bijar, consisted of 'A' and 'D' Squadrons, and supporting arms. Some 150 Turkish cavalry were reported to be south of Kara Bulagh, near Bijar. Regular patrols were sent out and attacks were expected from the north and from the direction of Senna. But once the Turks had collapsed in Palestine, the operational situation changed. On 28 October, the Turkish Army was defeated at Sharqat in Mesopotamia, 5,000 prisoners were taken and an armistice with Turkey was signed.

This ended the *14th Hussars'* war in Persia, and by the end of December the Regiment was back in Mesopotamia.

FRANCE 1918

Following the Revolution in 1917, Russia ceased to pose a threat to Germany, and this meant that more German troops were available to reinforce the Western Front. In March 1918, the spring offensive or '*Kaiserschlacht*' began. The *20th* dismounted company, under Captain D'Arcy Hall, was sent to Vermand, west of St-Quentin, to help build a strong defensive position. It subsequently marched south to le Quesnoy, and on 14 March, the 5th Cavalry Brigade was reorganised as 5th Dismounted Brigade Group, rather than as a dismounted battalion, under Lieutenant-Colonel George Cook, and was warned to prepare for a German attack. As the front came under a heavy bombardment, Cook deployed his force to Lizerolles, and covered the withdrawal of the 43rd Infantry Brigade. On the 22nd the battalion withdrew and marched to Faillouel in readiness for a counter-attack from across the St-Quentin Canal. At 0800 on the 23rd the enemy reached the railway south of Jussy. Later, Major Arthur Little took stragglers from various units into positions along the Faillouel–Flavy-le-Martel road; squadrons from the Scots Greys, 12th Lancers and other regiments joined him. With this small 'army' he prepared to counter-attack, but abandoned the idea because of the sheer weight of numbers threatening his left flank. After holding the road for two hours, the battalion concentrated at Faillouel, and contact was established with the battalion on the right. The left flank was open, however, and the Germans sent a large number of infantry through it so a withdrawal was ordered. In this confused situation, the Regiment continued to retire in a somewhat exhausted condition.

At midnight on 24 March, on reaching Noyon, mounted regiments were formed from each brigade, the one from 5th Brigade being under Major Arthur Little. These regiments, under command of the Colonel, and known as 'Cook's Detachment', joined 3rd Cavalry Division, at Lagny on 25 March. At first the detachment was dismounted and took over front-line trenches, but the French needed support, so the Regiment found its horses, mounted and moved to Cartigny. On the 26th they moved to an isolated position between Dives and Lassigny. At 0930 the detachment crossed the Divette stream and, with some French troops, held the line of a wood north of Cuy. After the French withdrew, the *20th* and a 16th Lancers squadron advanced through Lagny and took up dismounted positions.

The Germans penetrated a gap to the north, so it was necessary to withdraw to a position covering the crossings over the Divette at Dives. But the enemy was again able to get round the left flank, and a further retirement was ordered to Thiescourt. During this withdrawal, the *20th* came under heavy artillery fire, suffering casualties, including Colonel George Cook who was killed. With his death the Regiment lost a sound and fearless leader. Lieutenant-Colonel Arthur Little assumed command, and the *20th* moved south to Arsy.

While the Dismounted Company was in action around Dives, Captain D'Arcy Hall was in command of the mounted element of the Regiment; he deployed 'C' Squadron, to a defensive position to the east at the Larbroye brickworks, and then moved south to Passel. The Regiment was ordered to seize and hold Hill 160 but this was impossible so it reinforced another squadron short of the hill, losing few casualties.

On 29 March 5th Cavalry Brigade marched to billets near Amiens, and next day to Bois l'Abbé. On the 31st a dismounted company, under Captain D'Arcy Hall, was formed as part of 5th Dismounted Battalion, with orders to counter-attack 'Rifle Wood', east of Domart-sur-la-Luce, early next day. The objective was a ridge sloping up from the Luce stream. Short of the wood, a sunken lane marked the start-line for the attack. Unfortunately on crossing it the

Regiment came under enfilade fire and suffered heavy casualties including three of the officers, though not Hall, who led his troops on to the objective. In hand-to-hand fighting, the position was successfully taken, and Hall's Spanish revolver, recently acquired in Amiens, accounted for several of the enemy. The Regiment was relieved at 2330, having had three men killed and three officers and 39 men wounded.

On 2 April, 5th Cavalry Brigade were withdrawn and refitted. On the 9th the Germans started a new offensive, and 5th Cavalry Brigade was put at two hours' notice to re-deploy. On the 13th the Regiment marched to Hézecques and then on to la Belle-Hôtesse, north of the Forêt de Nieppe, where it had last been in October 1914. The front line was now close to Vieux Berquin, which was crowded with refugees. The Cavalry Division was detailed to protect First Army's left flank; the Regiment patrolled the Forêt de Nieppe. On 5 May the *20th* went back to Aix-en-Issart, east of le Touquet. The summer was spent on reorganisation, training, and sport; by August the Regiment was ready for whatever was to follow.

On 3 August, after a race meeting run by a Tank Corps unit, at which Lieutenant Colin Davy won a mile flat race, a 'secret' message was received that 5th Cavalry Brigade was to march the next day. Like all such plans, even today, the Motor Transport Troop had heard the news two days before. The *20th*, thirsting for battle and marching by night, arrived at Ailly-sur-Somme on the 7th, moved through Amiens, arrived at Glisy at 0430 next day, and then advanced to Cachy.

On 8 August, General Rawlinson launched British Fourth Army with French First Army against the German Eighteenth and Second Armies over a front of eleven miles in the Second Battle of Amiens. A preliminary bombardment by 2,070 guns was followed through by thirteen divisions and more tanks than had ever been used before. The recently formed Royal Air Force carried out artillery observation and ground-support tasks. When the battle ended on 4 September, the Germans had sustained more than 100,000 casualties; Allied losses were 22,000 British and 20,000 French. General von Ludendorff, then German Commander on the Western Front, described 8 August as the 'Black Day' of the German Army.

At 1145 on the 8th, the *20th* crossed the Luce to the south at Ignaucourt, passing large numbers of enemy dead, abandoned guns and vehicles. Next day the Brigade, now under the Canadian Corps, marched east to Beaucourt, and *20th* patrols reported enemy between le Quenel and Beaufort. The *20th* advanced on the left, with Beaufort as their objective; on the right were the Greys whose objective was le Quenel. 'C' Squadron, under Captain John Darling, was in the lead. Lieutenant Charles Mann and his troop galloped across 300 yards of open ground on their magnificent chestnut horses, but many were hit as the troop came under heavy machine-gun fire, though happily the men were unscathed. The Colonel ordered the squadron into a gully for cover, but it was occupied by tanks and infantry forming up to attack the village. The squadron withdrew, and the only casualty was Darling, the squadron leader, who was slightly wounded by a shell and gassed, but was fit enough to return home next day to get married.

On the 10th the Regiment was relieved, and the 5th Cavalry Brigade concentrated near Cayeux-en-Santerre. For the rest of the month, the Regiment was split up as divisional cavalry, patrolling in support of different formations. During this unspectacular period, some casualties were suffered, and the gas-contaminated ground prevented the horses from grazing. By the end of the month, the Regiment had

Left: Major Arthur Little (left), awarded a bar to his DSO after taking under command an ad hoc company to fill a gap in the front line. When Colonel Cook was killed, Little commanded the 20th Hussars. On the right is RSM Rabjohn of the 20th, who was awarded the MC during the war

concentrated at Warlincourt, north-east of Amiens, then moved to Béhencourt until 26 September, when they left for the last offensive.

While the Americans and Australians were attacking the Hindenberg Line east of Roisel, the *20th* crossed the Somme Canal at Brie and stayed at Mesnil Bruntel until 29 September. They then moved on to an assembly area at Hargicourt, west of the St-Quentin Canal. The Regiment was in an area heavily contaminated by gas shells.

One troop of 'C' Squadron and most of the Sergeants' Mess suffered severely from gas poisoning, having drunk tea made with water from a shell-hole.

On 30 September, the Regiment marched to a valley north-west of le Verguier, and a denuded 'C' Squadron was attached to 32nd Division onto high ground west of Bellenglise. On 1 October, orders for an attack on a trench line south of Joncourt were received. The initial infantry attack was successful, and three strong patrols under Lieutenant Charles Mann, SSM Adams and Sergeant Brook, were sent south-west of Ramicourt. Adams's patrol came under heavy fire as it tried gallantly to cross the trenches, but the brave attempt was to no avail, and every man was wounded.

On 3 October the *20th* marched to Présselles, in support of 46th Division. In the afternoon, the Germans counterattacked Montbrehain, and during shelling, Lieutenant Charles Mann was killed, and several other officers wounded or gassed. That evening Colonel Arthur Little formed a dismounted battalion from the 5th Cavalry Brigade and occupied a line east of Présselles. On 12 October, the brigade was split up, and the *20th* were sent to Bohain as corps cavalry under the American II Corps, but there were few opportunities for using it in its mounted role. On 21 October, the *20th* were concentrated around Vaux-le-Pretre, and temporarily rejoined 5th Cavalry Brigade.

On 5 November, the Regiment, now under 97th Infantry Brigade, marched north-east to Bazuel and passed through the leading brigades after the divisional

Left: RSM Goddard of the 14th was awarded the MC during the war (Norwyn Photographics)

attack on the Sambre and Oise Canal. 'C' Squadron took part in the subsequent advance, two troops, under Captain Sparrow, were with the Argyll and Sutherland Highlanders on the left and two other troops, under Lieutenant Bland, with the Border Regiment on the right. Sparrow's troops reached Maroilles and, although stopped by heavy machine-gun fire, captured three prisoners. On the right, Bland took le Favril, capturing two 8in guns, 29 prisoners and the affections of the prettiest girl in the village, who was seen with her arms clasped round him. Disappointingly for him, he had to tear himself away and resume the advance for a further two miles until held up by machine-gun fire. At noon, the remainder of the Regiment reached le Favril, and on 7 November, as the advance continued, the *20th* were held up by machine-gun fire a mile short of Avesnes. SSM Adams, leading a patrol, galloped into a party of enemy, was wounded and captured. There were other casualties, including the Medical Officer and one man killed.

On 8 November, 'B' Squadron sent out patrols, under Lieutenants Michell and Ralli to Avesnes and reported that it had now been evacuated. On return, while passing a burning railway ammunition wagon, it blew up, fatally wounding Ralli and two of his men. On 9 November, the *20th* passed through the infantry at Pont-de-la-Ville and reached the eastern edge of their battle maps. They were five miles ahead of the nearest infantry, out of touch with the flanking units but in contact with the enemy three miles ahead at Touvent. Colonel Arthur Little was temporarily in command of the 5th Cavalry Brigade, and Major Sanford was in command of the Regiment.

On 10 November, dawn patrols found a strong German machine-gun position north-west of Eppe Sauvage. Later, orders were given for the *20th* to form an advance-guard for a move to the north-east of the Bois de Touvent. On the left the 12th Lancers were held up by machine-gun fire at Sivry which stopped any further advance. Although the Regiment was over the Belgian border, it withdrew for the last night of the war to Clairfayts, a mile from the German front line.

On 11 November, after receiving a warning of the impending Armistice, orders were given to advance as far as possible so that further ground might be secured before hostilities ended. Lieutenants Dawnay and Burt went forward with their troops to carry this out, and the latter was actually stalking a German machine-gun when the cease-fire was declared at 1100.

The First World War was enormously important in the histories of both the *14th King's Hussars* and the *20th Hussars*. Although the *14th* had to wait until 1915 for action, their participation in the Mesopotamian campaign and subsequent operations in Persia were crucial to the protection of the oilfields. The *20th Hussars* were among the first British troops to engage the Germans in 1914, and they were still in contact when the Armistice was announced in 1918. Both regiments were well rewarded for their services; the *14th* received five battle honours, and the *20th* ten. A significant number of DSOs, DCMs, MCs and MMs were awarded to members of both regiments, including a DSO and Bar to Lieutenant-Colonel Arthur Little of the *20th*, MCs to the two RSMs, Goddard of the *14th* and Rabjohn of the *20th*. But there was a price to pay in casualties: the *14th* lost fourteen officers and 130 men killed and the *20th*, thirteen officers and 187 men killed, including two commanding officers, Lieutenant-Colonels Robert Hewitt of the *14th* and George Cook of the *20th*.

10 AMALGAMATION AND MECHANISATION

In February 1919, part of the *14th (King's) Hussars* joined a Composite Cavalry Regiment with the 7th and 13th Hussars, commanded by Captain M. J. Ambler as an Acting Lieutenant-Colonel, and stayed in the theatre. The remainder became a cadre, sailed from Basra on 25 March on an uneventful voyage home, except that one of the ship's Indian crewman died of bubonic plague. After disembarking at Liverpool, the cadre joined the 2nd Cavalry Brigade at Tidworth.

On 15 May Lieutenant-Colonel R. V. K. Applin took over command; this did not stop his contesting a seat at the Dartford by-election, though he lost. In November, the King presented decorations, won in the war, to seven officers and to RSM Goddard. A draft of 378 men was sent to the *20th Hussars*, and in November 1920, the *14th* left for Cologne; in March 1921, at short notice, they were ordered to occupy Düsseldorf where they remained for two months. In June, 'A' Squadron, under Major M. J. Ambler, was ordered to join an Allied force in Silesia where fighting had broken out between the Poles and Germans; they returned to Cologne a year later.

In the meantime the *20th Hussars*, home in March 1919, sailed for Egypt in July under Lieutenant-Colonel M. C. Richardson. In defiance of the Peace Conference, which had re-drawn the map of Europe, Turkish nationalists rebelled and concentrated around Ismit. A British contingent was sent to join the Army of the Black Sea, to enforce the Peace Treaty. The *20th* left Egypt and arrived at

Above: Soldiers in the 20th Hussars, off duty at the Pyramids, before leaving Egypt to carry out the 'Last Cavalry Charge' in Turkey

Opposite page: A 14th King's Hussars recruiting poster of 1921 (Norwyn Photographics)

Deringe on 20 July 1920. The Turks had by now advanced along the coast of the peninsula, taken Gebze and blown the bridge. A detachment consisting of the *20th Hussars*, 2/39 Royal Garhwal Rifles, and supporting arms was sent to evict the Turks. The *20th* were drawn up on the enemy's right flank while the Garwhalis attacked. As the Turks took up prepared positions in front of the village, at 1,000 yards, the *20th* prepared to charge. After the artillery barrage the *20th* advanced, two squadrons forward and one in reserve. Nearly 300 cavalrymen pressed on towards the enemy, swords drawn, and trumpets sounding. As the artillery barrage lifted, the *20th* charged the Turkish position, regrouped and galloped back through the position again. Within the space of thirty minutes the Turks had fled, and the last regimental cavalry charge in military history had been a complete success. Although the Nationalists stood their ground, they had many casualties; the only casualty in the *20th* was Lieutenant Leslie Groves, who was hit in the knee.

Despite the uncertain political situation world wide, the British government decided to reduce the size of the Army. The eight junior line cavalry regiments, including the *20th*, were warned for disbandment. Drafts were transferred to the 3rd Hussars and to the *11th Hussars*. The remainder of the Regiment returned to England, under Lieutenant-Colonel Arthur Little, to prepare for disbandment. However, as military commitments in India, the Middle East and Ireland remained, all was not lost. In January 1922, the *20th Hussars*, now reduced to a cadre of seven all ranks, was told that the War Office would preserve its name. One squadron would be resuscitated, amalgamate with the *14th King's Hussars*, and wear its former uniform. On 1 October 1922, the Regiment became the *14th/20th Hussars*, the title *King's* being dropped until 1936. The *Prussian Eagle*, which reappeared in 1926, was not officially authorised as a cap badge until 1931.

In October 1923, the *14th/20th* returned home to Aliwal Barracks, Tidworth and joined the 2nd Cavalry Brigade with the 12th and 17th/21st Lancers. However, time had started to influence modern warfare. As armoured fighting vehicles came into service the demise of the horse could be foreseen. Nevertheless the Regiment made the most of its sporting prowess. Captain Alf Sturt, who was an exceptional horseman, having joined the *20th* as a private, had many show-jumping successes, and, with Lieutenant Johnny Pemberton, reached the final of the Prince of Wales's Cup at Olympia. All cavalry officers hunted, played polo, and led hectic social lives. Such

an existence was expensive, but less so in the *14th/20th* than elsewhere; it was rumoured that an officer in the 17th/21st Lancers had been forced to transfer to the Grenadier Guards to economise.

The Regiment helped build the Fisher Polo Ground, named after the Brigade Commander, and maintained its reputation for marksmanship by winning seven cups and 89 medals in the Army Rifle Association Competition. The Commanding Officer, Lieutenant-Colonel John Hurndall, who had won the MC in the *20th* during the Great War, was now a nine goal handicap polo player and captained the English team in America for the Westchester Cup. At the brigade horse show, a team in the Sword, Lance and Revolver Competition, comprising SQMS Wash and SSM 'Bunny' Trueman, was particularly successful. Trueman had won the MM with the *20th* on the Hindenburg Line, was later RSM and was to become a Lieutenant-Colonel during the Second World War; he achieved seven show-jumping wins, as did Lieutenant Johnny Pemberton, who had two at the International Horse Show at Nice and five others elsewhere.

In 1924, the rank of Private in the Cavalry of the Line, used for three centuries, was redesignated as Trooper. The *14th/20th* moved to York in 1926 at a strength of 27 officers, and 539 men, but with only 393 horses, as experimental mechanisation was beginning. 'C' Squadron was temporarily dismounted and converted to a machine-gun squadron. In October 1929, the Regiment, under Lieutenant-Colonel Geoffrey Darley left York for Aldershot, 25 men overstrength; the turn-out of men and horses at public displays indicated how high the morale was in the *14th/20th Hussars*. In 1929 SSM 'Bunny' Trueman won eleven first prizes on 'Lapwing' and in 1928 Captain Gerald Poole won the Foxhunter Steeplechase on 'Pippins II' over the

Above: Lieutenant Johnny Pemberton showjumping at Nice (Norwyn Photographics; courtesy Major Andrew Pemberton)

Above right: Troop Sergeant-Major John Stratford, a Ramnuggur veteran, at Tidworth in 1924 (Steve Day; courtesy The King's Royal Hussars)

Below right: Stratford's military funeral at Wolverhampton in 1932 (Courtesy Douglas Hill)

98

Grand National Course, the only member of the *14th/20th* ever to ride a winner at Liverpool.

In October 1930, the Regiment marched to Hounslow, and in September 1931 sailed for Egypt and established itself in Abbassia Barracks near Cairo. The *14th/20th* was again in the same brigade as the 12th and 17th/21st Lancers. The 1st Battalion, the Royal Warwickshire Regiment, under Lieutenant-Colonel Bernard Montgomery, were based at Alexandria. Although only a lieutenant-colonel, 'Monty' was already making an impression locally both with his superiors and with the other regiments, not always a favourable one. While he approved of the 12th Lancers, who had mechanised with the *11th Hussars*, being the two most junior non-amalgamated regiments, '... he thought the cavalry were a nonsense, not serious soldiers, just there for hunting, polo and fishing. He told them so.'* While the Regiment's name is not specifically mentioned in this account, it was felt that this untimely acquaintance with Monty may have had some influence on its exclusion from both the Desert and Western Europe until the close of the Second World War.

On 16 January 1932, the last survivor of the Battle of *Ramnuggur*, and a veteran of the Second Sikh War, Persia and the Indian Mutiny, Troop-Sergeant-Major John Stratford, died at Wolverhampton, aged 102. He was buried with full military honours, and the Staffordshire Yeomanry provided a bearer party. A

tablet to his memory was erected in St Peter's Church, Wolverhampton.

In 1933, Adolf Hitler became Chancellor of Germany, and the move towards war had begun. The *14th/20th Hussars* sailed for India and arrived at Risalpur in January 1934. They were brought up to the Indian establishment of 572 men and 559 troop horses, and the Regiment was fully mounted once more. Major 'Darky' Pope took over as Master of the Risalpur Hounds, which had nineteen couple.

In October 1936 the Regiment moved to Lucknow, and the Adjutant, Captain Gerald Chaytor, took over the Lucknow Hounds. After hunting them for the season, he was killed playing polo in the Inter-Regimental, the second *14th/20th* officer to die on the polo field in India; the first being Captain R. H. Hannay, two years earlier. That same year, contrary to the Treaty of Versailles, German forces re-entered the demilitarised Rhineland, and Italy invaded Abyssinia. Neither event made much impression on the

* Hamilton, Nigel. *Monty – The Making of a General*, p.99.

Above: *All India Boxing Champions 1937. Left to right: top, Trooper Volley (Welter), Mr MacFarlaine (Trainer), Trooper Hill (Heavy); bottom, Trooper Wood (Feather), Lance-Corporal Draper (Fly), Trooper Emslie (Bantam) and Trooper Leese (Light). Douglas 'Tiny' Hill has been the Regimental Historian since 1982* (Norwyn Photographics; courtesy Douglas Hill)

Below: *The final mounted parade of the 14th/20th King's Hussars before mechanisation, at Lucknow in August 1938. The band is on the right of the picture, mounted on grey horses* (Courtesy Douglas Hill)

Above: *Signals Troop at Lucknow–Trimulgherry, 1937–1938. Left to right, standing: back row, Trooper Westall, Trooper Battye, Trooper Watts, Trooper Mann; standing: centre row, Trooper Cranston, Trooper Wretham, Trooper Cameron, Trooper McEwan, Trooper Bell, Trooper Wassell, Trooper Craig, Trooper Callaghan, Trooper McCleave; standing: front row, Trooper Worsdell, Trooper Urquhart, Trooper Chalmers, Trooper Bennett, Trooper Bourne, Trooper Hardy, Trooper Ramsay, Trooper Bootle, Trooper West, Trooper Flood; seated, Lance-Corporal Cunningham, Lance-Corporal Grant, Lance-Corporal Tulloch, Lance-Corporal Stanley, Corporal Neatham, Lieutenant P. F. S. Haggie, Corporal St. Pierre, Corporal Gower, Lance-Corporal Bayliss, Lance-Corporal Mulraney, Trooper Kay. At the left and right front of the picture are two of the troop's heliographs, which communicated by reflecting flashes of sunlight* (Norwyn Photographics; courtesy Lieutenant-Colonel Rollo Clifford)

British government nor on public opinion, because Great Britain and the Empire were distracted by the abdication of King Edward VIII. George VI was proclaimed King Emperor in Lucknow on 14 December 1936, and two days later the Regiment was re-designated the *14th/20th King's Hussars*. While on the frontier and at Lucknow, experimental training took place co-operating with tanks, lorried infantry and motor transport, under the new commanding officer, Lieutenant-Colonel 'Darky' Pope.

Despite the versatility of horses, everyone knew that mechanisation loomed. In February 1938, Germany occupied Austria, and Hitler announced his plans to liberate the Sudetenland part of Czechoslovakia. The seemingly weak diplomacy on the part of Great Britain did however avoid war for a while and bought time to re-arm. The infamous Munich Agreement signed by Hitler and Chamberlain, for which the latter attracted so much criticism, may have been wiser than it seemed.

As the need for armour became apparent, there was a strong case for expanding the Royal Tank Corps, but the regimental system was to preserve the Cavalry.

Below: Lieutenant-Colonel Leslie Groves and Captain Basil Woodd inspect a newly arrived Mark VIB Tank. (The Colonel appears to have recovered from his wounds sustained during the 'Last Cavalry Charge' in 1920)

Bottom: The first mechanised mounted parade at Secunderabad in 1938 (Norwyn Photographics)

Mechanisation began in earnest in 1937, and in January 1938 the *14th/20th* went out training on horseback for the last time. In August the Regiment said good-bye to its horses, apart from officers' chargers, and in November the first Vickers tanks arrived with a training team, under Captain L. C. Rumsey, from the Royal Tank Corps; apparently, no officer spoke to him for a week.

On 31 March 1939, the *14th/20th King's Hussars*, now at Secunderabad, were officially converted to a mechanised regiment. Ten days later all ranks were transferred from the Cavalry of the Line to the Royal Armoured Corps. On 1 September, the German Army invaded Poland, and on 3 September 1939, Great Britain declared war on Germany.

11

THE SECOND WORLD WAR

When war was declared on 3 September 1939, the British Army was dispersed world wide with the role of defending the Empire. In the Middle East there were some six infantry divisions whose tasks were to ensure access to the Suez Canal and to protect the oilfields. In Malaya there were only two brigades, and in India, troops were also scarce. When it was decided to send the British Expeditionary Force (BEF) from the United Kingdom to France, only four infantry divisions were available.

Like the *14th* in 1914, the *14th/20th King's Hussars* were still in India, but now fully mechanised with Mark VI light tanks and Bren-gun carriers. They moved to Meerut in October 1939, and in January 1940 Lieutenant-Colonel Leslie Groves

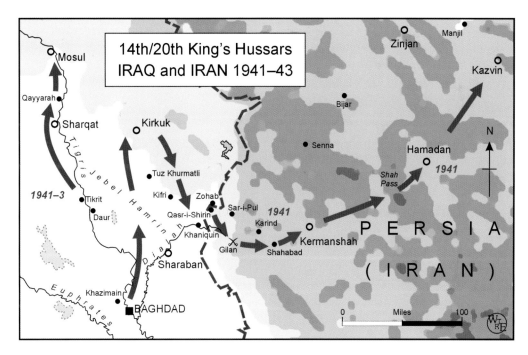

assumed command. In February 1941 a contingent of nine officers and 102 men, under Lieutenant-Colonel John Norton, was sent to the recently formed *26th Hussars*, whose adjutant was Captain Anthony Stanton, a Sword of Honour winner at Sandhurst, sadly to be killed later in New Guinea. (The decision to resurrect the *26th Hussars* with five other cavalry regiments disbanded in the nineteenth century was questioned by Churchill who felt that the 1922 amalgamations should have been reversed instead.)

In March 1941, the pro-German prime minister of Iraq overthrew the Regent, had his troops surround the RAF Station at Habbaniya and threatened to cut the oil pipeline from Kirkuk to Haifa. After reinforcements were flown in, the Iraqis withdrew, but hostile activities continued, and more troops were needed. The Regiment mobilised in May 1941, and on 24 June sailed from Bombay to Basra, with 2nd Indian Armoured Brigade.

The Regiment arrived in Basra on 3 July, and, after working for ten days in temperatures of 120° F (48° C), moved to Baghdad. On the journey, both Groves and his Adjutant, Captain R. J. W. McAllen, collapsed of heat stroke, and the latter died. On arrival in Iraq, the *14th/20th* moved to Kirkuk and then to Khaniquin. The force invading Persia was divided into two; the main body, under Brigadier Aizlewood, consisted of the Regiment, less 'C' Squadron, a battalion of Gurkhas and artillery. The second column, 'POCOL', under Aizlewood's deputy, Colonel Pocock, consisted of 'C' Squadron, part of 9th Armoured Brigade and artillery.

The Main Body crossed the Persian border and arrived at Qasr-i-Shirin early on 25 August. Half-way up the Pai-Tak Pass, Recce Troop came under heavy fire, and the axis of advance was changed to that of POCOL which had taken a southern route, east of Khaniquin. 'C' Squadron and two sections of Recce Troop, under Lieutenant Dickie Talbot, led, and turned south-east for Gilan. Recce Troop came under heavy fire and went to ground. Pocock ordered Captain 'Bodge' Browne forward with two troops, under Lieutenants Donovan and Campbell, in line ahead. They too were fired on, and as Donovan's tank was manoeuvring into position it got stuck.

Browne brought up a carrier, driven by SSM Senior, to tow him out. He dismounted under continuous small-arms fire, fixed the tow-rope and pulled the tank out. Then his carrier ran out of petrol and had to be towed away by Donovan. 'C' Squadron was then withdrawn to a harbour. This encounter was to be described in *Victor* comic entitled 'A True Story of Men at War', in 1978. There were some similarities in Browne's bravery here to that of Major Edward Brown at Geluk in 1900, for which he won the VC.* Captain 'Bodge' Browne was awarded an immediate MC for this action and Lieutenant Talbot was 'Mentioned in Despatches'.

Above: Extract from the Victor *comic of 1978 showing Captain Browne's exploit in Persia (© D. C. Thomson & Co., Ltd.)*

*Oatts, L. B. *The Emperor's Chambermaids*

The enemy evacuated their positions, and, despite a blown bridge, the Regiment reached Shahabad on 27 August. Next day, 'B' Squadron, under Major Chris Johnston, brother of Brian Johnston the BBC cricket commentator, prepared to attack the main Persian position, but unexpectedly, the enemy surrendered. There was a victory march through Kermanshah on 30 August, after which the *14th/20th* advanced over the Shah Pass to Hamadan, to an enthusiastic welcome. During the move, over six days, the Regiment drove 350 miles, lost one tank to enemy fire, and only five broke down. In such difficult country, this seviceability seems to have been a reasonable achievement compared with what can be managed now. During this advance, the Brigadier and Major Bob Stephen, escorted by a company of Gurkhas, left for Kazvin to make the first official contact between British and Russian troops of the war. The language problem was alleviated during a lunch accompanied by liberal

Right: The 14th/20th King's Hussars enter Kermanshah. (Tank Museum, Bovington)

quantities of vodka. This ended the successful Iraq and Persian campaigns, and the third, but not the last, visit to that part of the world in the history of the Regiment.

On 23 October, the *14th/20th* left Hamadan for Quayyara, on the Tigris. In March 1942, the Regiment moved to Mosul, and in June to Bitsun where it re-equipped before returning to Basra in November. On 12 January 1943, Lieutenant-Colonel 'Freckles' Tilney assumed command, the second generation of four to serve in the *14th, 14th/20th* and now *The King's Royal Hussars*.

In October 1943, the Regiment left for Burg-el-Arab near Alexandria. While it was to enjoy near civilisation, an intensive period of re-equipment and infantry/tank training took place. In March 1944, the *14th/20th* moved to Qatana, near Damascus to continue its training, but this was cut short when a 700-mile forced march to Alexandria was ordered. It had been hoped that this was the precursor to eagerly awaited active service, but it was only to put down a local disturbance; Monty's scourge had yet to be lifted.

Above left: 2nd Troop 'C' Squadron in Syria, 1944. Left to right: back row, Troopers Mabbs, Hall, Grantham, Fowler, Whear, Henley Stalker; front row, Troopers Germain, Murray, Sergeant Barnes, Lieutenant Burgham, Sergeant Higgenbottom, Corporal Bennett, Lance-Corporal Cowling (Courtesy Russell Burgham)

Above left:
Lieutenant-Colonel David Silvertop, killed commanding 3RTR in Holland in 1944 (Steve Day; courtesy The King's Royal Hussars)

Above: *Captain George Sullivan (second from left) with the Trans-Jordan Frontier Force*

Above right: *Left to right: Major Jock Mann, 'B' Squadron Leader, Captain Brian Tayleur, Adjutant, Major 'Bodge' Browne, 'C' Squadron Leader, and Major Bob Stephen, Second-in-Command, in Italy, 1945*

Below left: *Recce Troop in their 'Indian Type' armoured wheeled carriers in the Middle East in 1942 (Tank Museum, Bovington)*

While the Regiment was in waiting, one officer, Major David Silvertop, was particularly successful. While Brigade Major of 4th Armoured Brigade, he was awarded the MC, and later commanded the 3rd Royal Tank Regiment in North Africa and North West Europe. He was conspicuous during Operation 'Goodwood', and 3RTR played a leading role in the liberation of Antwerp. He was awarded the DSO on the recommendation of the Commander of 29th Armoured Brigade, Brigadier Rosco Harvey of the *10th Royal Hussars*. Sad to tell, Silvertop was killed in Holland in September 1944. While commanding 3RTR, he visited the Regiment in Alexandria, dressed as a major of the *14th/20th* complete with red side hat. He told the Colonel that if he needed a squadron leader, he would gladly relinquish his higher rank and return. Major George Sullivan also had an interesting war. He served first with the Trans Jordan Frontier Force in Syria, and later with the East Riding Yeomanry; in October 1944 he was wounded and captured, but escaped three times, the last time successfully; he was awarded the MC.

At the end of 1944, the Regiment was ordered to take part in the Italian campaign. An advance-party, under Major Eddie Studd, left on Christmas Day, and the main body of the *14th/20th King's Hussars* arrived at Taranto, on 21 January 1945. On 31 January, 'B' Squadron, under Major Jock Mann, occupied a position 60 miles north of Florence and was in action in an artillery role. The remainder left for San Donato on 1 February.

Before the spring offensive began, the *14th/20th* were withdrawn to Cesena, west of Rimini, where 'A' Squadron was converted from Sherman tanks to Kangaroo Armoured Personnel Carriers (APCs). The Regiment was then to join the 43rd Gurkha Lorried Infantry Brigade, under Brigadier 'Tochi' Barker. The Brigade also comprised, *2nd/6th*, 2nd/8th and 2nd/10th Gurkha Rifles, 2nd Royal Tank Regiment (RTR), 'R' Battery 15 Medium Regiment RA, 25 Field Regiment RA, 78 (*Duke of Lancaster's Own Yeomanry*) Medium Regiment RA, one battery Polish Self-Propelled (SP) anti-tank guns and one assault squadron RE. It was in II Polish Corps, and part of Eighth Army, commanded by General Sir Richard McCreery.

The Corps' intention was to make a frontal assault over the rivers Senio and Santerno, north-east of the main Rimini–Modena road. The 43rd Brigade was to exploit the Corps' break-in and take the road communications centre at Medicina. The Corps attacked across the river Senio at 1900 on 9 April, after a heavy aerial

Right: Lieutenant-Colonel 'Freckles' Tilney, in command of the Regiment at the Battle of Medicina

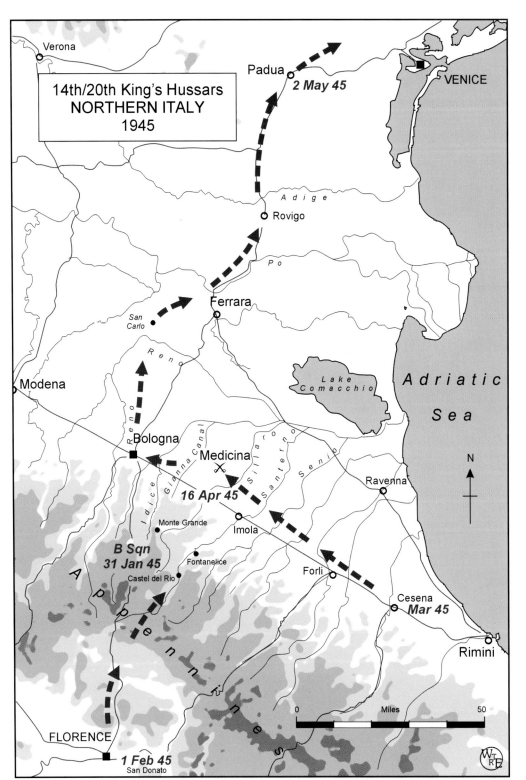

Right: Major 'Bodge' Browne, 'C' Squadron Leader at Medicina and awarded an immediate DSO. He was one of several members of the Regiment to be decorated after the battle (Steve Day)

bombardment. Progress was slow against fierce opposition and it took five days to get across the Santerno.

The *14th/20th King's Hussars* Regimental Group's plan was for 'A' Squadron 2 RTR to cross the Sillaro first, and act as left flank guard. 'C' Squadron was to cross next and form the Regiment's advance-guard, with one troop from 'A' Squadron *14th/20th*, carrying 'A' Company *2/6 GR*. 'B' Squadron formed the main body and escorted the remainder of the Kangaroos. The crossing started at 0945 am on 16 April.

In the close country of thick vineyards and orchards, intersected by ditches and canals, which proved to be minor tank obstacles, progress was slow. 1st Troop, 'C' Squadron led, until it met its first opposition from the German 124th Infantry Regiment supported by 105mm SP guns, and the troop leader, Lieutenant George Camburn, was wounded. At about 0011, 2nd Troop, under Lieutenant Russell Burgham, then took over the lead. Major Browne called over the radio: 'You know what to do, whips out!' The squadron raced through the vineyards, firing as it moved. Lance-Sergeant Higgenbottom's tank was hit by a shell and immediately brewed up. The co-driver, Trooper Murray, was trapped in the fire and killed. As Burgham's tank pulled up by a farmhouse, it was hit from behind by a bazooka and put out of action; the bazooka operator was killed by supporting fire. More Germans emerged from dug-outs and were taken prisoner. The troop sergeant, Sergeant Henry Hall, pressed on towards the town until his tank was hit five times, but he continued to engage the enemy until he could fire no more; Hall then dismounted and carried on the battle from another tank. For his determination, leadership and example he was given an immediate award of the DCM.

At 1815 'C' Squadron and 'A' Squadron 2 RTR were halted two miles short of Medicina. Brigadier Barker arrived at RHQ and told the Colonel that as enemy resistance seemed to be crumbling, the time was ripe to attack. 'C' Squadron was therefore ordered to advance on Medicina with all speed in the remaining hour of good daylight; 'A' Squadron 2RTR would continue to guard the left flank.

In the failing light, Major 'Bodge' Browne led the Squadron down the Via Saffi, saying over the radio: 'Let's show them a good old cavalry charge, fingers out and follow me!' At about 2000 he burst into the centre of the town down the only unblocked road, with all guns blazing. He destroyed a 105mm SP gun which was facing him, but the exploding ammunition around the gun brought down a house behind him. At the same time, SSM Long, in the next SHQ tank, was killed by a sniper. Browne drove on, dispersed the crews of two 88mm guns and reached the station square. Here his tank was hit by a bazooka and set on fire. His gunner, Trooper Burt was killed, his operator Sergeant Evans was burned and Major Browne was seriously wounded in the leg, but was given an immediate award of the DSO. His driver, Trooper Armstrong, and co-driver, Lance-Corporal McGregor, dismounted and killed the various bazooka teams. Armstrong then returned to help the tank crew and McGregor reported back to RHQ, on foot; both men were given immediate awards of the MM. After Browne was wounded, Captain Douglas Heath, took over command of 'C' Squadron and secured the town, for which he was awarded an immediate MC. Lieutenant Ken Brailey, as a Kangaroo Troop Leader, fired at snipers with his .50 Browning, after the Gurkhas had dismounted and evacuated the wounded, for which he too was awarded an immediate MC.

In bad light, the Germans had thought that the Kangaroo APCs were tanks, and were convinced that they were about to be overwhelmed. The Brigadier's judgement of poor enemy morale had clearly proved to be correct. After the APCs had been escorted to dismounting points, the fighting intensified from all parts of the town. The Gurkhas were engaged in hand-to-hand fighting, clearing the houses and those strong-points the Germans were occupying. 'B' Squadron took up counter-attack positions for the night. Next day a number of prisoners were rounded up, some

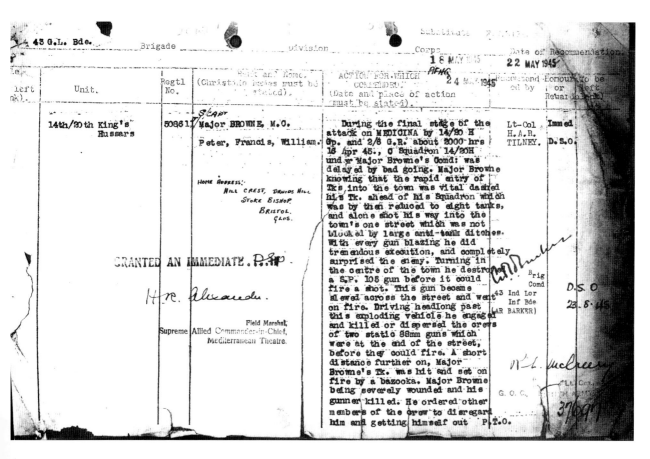

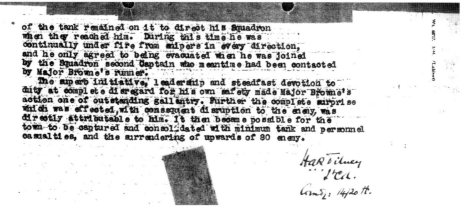

Left: *The Battle of Medicina, by Bryan de Grineau* (Illustrated London News)

This page: *Major Browne's citation for the DSO*

showing short-lived arrogance, but most were in shock. Medicina, however, had been 'C' Squadron's day.

After this, 43 Brigade was put under command of the New Zealand Division, which itself had been planning a divisional attack. Major-General Freyberg, the Divisional Commander, told the Brigadier that his Brigade was the only one the New Zealanders had admired from behind. The *14th/20th* Group continued the advance on 17 April, with 'A' Squadron 2 RTR in the lead. Opposition at the Gianna Canal was primarily taken on by *2/6 GR* in 'A' Squadron's APCs, who made two attacks, supported by the rest of the Regiment. These were only partially successful, and on 18 April, Freyberg planned a major assault to begin at 2200 on

the 19th. The *14th/20th* Group provided indirect fire, shooting a vast quantity of ammunition at ranges up to 13,000 yards. Next day the position was taken. Regimental losses were two killed and six wounded, and 43 Brigade was withdrawn behind Medicina.

On 22 April, Lieutenant-Colonel Bob Stephen took over command, and as the advance continued the Regiment was delayed on the river Po while tank bridges were built. On the 28th, Eighth Army ordered 'C' Squadron, now under Major Peter Clifford, to convert to APCs, as they were urgently needed on V Corps' front in the east. This required a march of 20 miles, handing in thirteen tanks, drawing 24 Kangaroos, fitting extra radios and reorganising the crews, which the Squadron achieved in 30 hours.

After crossing the Po, the Regiment was held up at the river Adige, which could only be negotiated by raft at the rate of six tanks an hour. When the *14th/20th* concentrated at Padua on 2 May 1945, all German forces in Italy had surrendered, and six days later, the war in Europe was over.

Despite earlier distinctions in its history, the Regiment carried out a comparatively small fighting part in the War and saw less action than other regular Royal Armoured Corps regiments; it felt deeply about this. It was only fortunate that casualties were modest: five officers and 25 men killed. However the inspired leadership of Major 'Bodge' Browne at Gilan and at Medicina maintained the Regiment's reputation. It is interesting that of the three battles celebrated annually, *RAMNUGGUR*, *RAMADI* and *MEDICINA*, only *MEDICINA* was awarded as a battle honour.

Above and above left: 4th Troop 'B' Squadron tank crew at Alexandria in 1943, and at the Medicina Reunion in 1995.
Left to right: Corporal Ron Barnard (Wireless Operator), Trooper Jack Crowe (Tank Driver), Sergeant Ken Dowding (Troop Sergeant), Trooper Les White (Tank Gunner) (Courtesy Ken Dowding)

Left: The Medicina Memorial (Courtesy Ken Dowding)

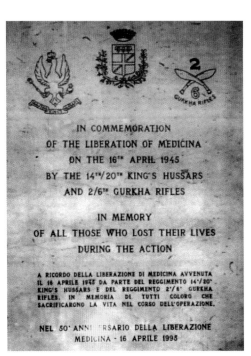

IN COMMEMORATION
OF THE LIBERATION OF MEDICINA
ON THE 16ᵀᴴ APRIL 1945
BY THE 14ᵀᴴ/20ᵀᴴ KING'S HUSSARS
AND 2/6ᵀᴴ GURKHA RIFLES

IN MEMORY
OF ALL THOSE WHO LOST THEIR LIVES
DURING THE ACTION

A RICORDO DELLA LIBERAZIONE DI MEDICINA AVVENUTA IL 16 APRILE 1945 DA PARTE DEL REGGIMENTO 14°/20° KING'S HUSSARS E DEL REGGIMENTO 2°/6° GURKHA RIFLES. IN MEMORIA DI TUTTI COLORO CHE SACRIFICARONO LA VITA NEL CORSO DELL'OPERAZIONE.

NEL 50° ANNIVERSARIO DELLA LIBERAZIONE
MEDICINA - 16 APRILE 1995

12

THE COLD WAR

The Yalta Conference in February 1945 is generally considered to mark the beginning of the Cold War. After hostilities with Germany ended, Allied and Soviet forces faced each other along the line of the 'Iron Curtain', which divided East and West Germany. The Regiment was to spend much of the following 45 years in the British Army of the Rhine (BAOR), at the hub of the Cold War, and close to the East German border. Allied forces needed to remain in Europe to restore normality, and in August 1945 the *14th/20th King's Hussars* moved to Chiavari, near Genoa, responsible for internal security. In 1946 they moved to Luneburg, and then Wuppertal in the Ruhr, starting a pattern of constant changes of station and task, equipped with either tanks or armoured cars, or in their training role in the UK.

In January 1947, the Brigade of Gurkhas approved the Regiment wearing the emblem of crossed kukris, as a badge, in recognition of their wartime comradeship with the Gurkhas. After mechanisation nine years earlier, equestrian ability had lapsed, so riding school was started again, and the Regiment took part in a Musical Ride at the Dortmund Tattoo with the Royal Horse Guards (The Blues). In the Arctic winter of 1946/47, skiing started at Winterberg, and Rugby football became popular. On 21 May 1947, General Sir Richard McCreery was appointed Colonel of the Regiment in succession to Brigadier John Hurndall. Although a 12th Lancer, he had been Hurndall's Brigade Major, when the latter commanded the 2nd Cavalry Brigade at Tidworth. In the Italian campaign, he commanded Eighth Army, and had counter-signed the citations for awards after Medicina. He was a logical choice as Colonel.

In May 1947, the first National Service Act was passed, followed a year later by the Soviet blockade of Berlin; the Regiment moved to Catterick, to train recruits. In October 1948, the Band, which had been the Mortar Troop during the war, was re-formed under Bandmaster Roy Hurst, and again became an indispensable part of regimental life. The Shooting Team won the Connaught Cup again, regimental horses won races at the Bedale point-to-point and did well in the modern pentathlon. The sporting high-

Below: The Regimental Football Team after winning the Cavalry Cup in 1950. Back row: Cpl Barden, Tprs Weaver, Lewing & Davey, Cpl Miller, Tpr Walker. Front Row: L/Cpl Townsley, Sgt Beaumont, Lt Hart, Cpl Bloomfield, Tpr Smith; and (bottom) a few hours later at the Old Comrades Reunion

light, however, was winning for the first time the Cavalry Cup Football Competition, 4–1, against the Scots Greys, on Leyton Orient's ground, on 29 April 1950.

With the outbreak of the Korean War, drafts were sent to regiments in the Commonwealth Brigade. Lieutenant Ted Paul, the nephew of Lieutenant Graham Paul the caricaturist in Persia during the First World War, was awarded the MC, while serving with the 8th Hussars. In July, the Peninsular Guidons of the *14th* and *20th Light Dragoons* were trooped, and when the Regiment left Catterick, it had trained 1,732 Regular and 6,167 National Service recruits, including 276 potential officers for entry to Sandhurst and Mons Officer Cadet School.

In January 1951, the Regiment left for Crookham, near Aldershot in Hampshire, where it took part in Exercise 'Surprise Packet', a major exercise over an area extending from Norfolk to Salisbury Plain. At the end of the year, Lieutenant-Colonel Basil Woodd, a four goal handicap polo player, and the fourth Carthusian, after Havelock, Hewitt and Hurndall, took command. In 1952, the *14th/20th* won ten cups, 39 medals and £40.00 in prize money at the Aldershot District Rifle Meeting. While presenting the awards, the CIGS, Field Marshal Sir William Slim, gave up shaking hands and just said: 'What you again'. In October the Regiment embarked for Tripoli in Libya, to a camp at Sabratha alongside the Roman amphitheatre. It was equipped with Centurion tanks, for possible use against Egypt, as hostilities between Jews and Arabs had intensified.

The Pentathlon Team won the Divisional Competition in which, despite protests, the cross-country riding test was on motor-cycles rather than horses. Polo was started again on the salt flats near Sabratha, and teams played in Malta. Officers and men rode polo ponies in flat races at Busetta, near Tripoli; the most successful being a lop-eared grey named 'Fileur', ridden by both Colonels Woodd and Allen, who never lost a race.

Top right: Field Marshal Sir William Slim presenting one of the ten cups, won by the 14th/20th, to Captain Peter Mossé at the Aldershot District Rifle Meeting in 1952

Centre right: The victorious team in the 1st Infantry Division Modern Pentathlon. Left to right: 2/Lt David Hume, Major Brian Tayleur and 2/Lt Peter Hicks

Below right: The Garian pass in Tripolitania

Bottom right: General Sir Richard McCreery (on the right), who became Colonel of the Regiment in 1947, with Lieutenant-Colonel Forty Allen at Piddlehinton in 1955

Left: The Parade at Catterick in July 1950, when the Peninsula Guidons were trooped. On the left is Lance-Corporal Bill Williams (**1**), who became Regimental Secretary in 1982. On the front left is Captain Peter Mossé (**2**), who became Chairman of the Regimental Association in 1991. Captain Douglas Heath (**3**) won the MC at Medicina

In 1954, Lieutenant-Colonel Forty Allen assumed command. He was a Cambridge graduate who, frustrated by lack of action in 1944, joined a battalion of the East Surrey Regiment, where he fought as an infantry officer. In January 1955 he took the entire Regiment up the Gebel escarpment, some 50 miles south of the Libyan coast, to train during an ambitious six-weeks' exercise, the brain child of Major Desmond Scarr. After the training ended, a national newspaper reported:

> "ROMMEL SAID
> IT'S IMPOSSIBLE, BUT
> British tanks have done something that Rommel said was impossible. They have climbed the narrow, steep and twisting road to the top of the 2,200-foot Garian Gebel plateau in Tripolitania. The two-mile road is edged on one side by rising rock, on the other by a sheer drop. This operation, one of the most difficult ever carried out by tanks of the peacetime Army, was undertaken by men of the 14/20 Hussars in Centurions."

In October, the Regiment returned home to Piddlehinton Camp in Dorset, for leave and recreation.

In March 1956, the *14th/20th King's Hussars* joined 20th Armoured Brigade at Münster, and Lieutenant-Colonel 'Bodge' Browne, the Regiment's hero during the war, assumed command. Browne was a regimental soldier through and through and had spent only three years away during his service. Administration was not to his liking, and he found peacetime regulations in BAOR, at best, irksome.

In November 1956 President Nasser nationalised the Suez Canal, and an Anglo-French force invaded Egypt. Three

14th/20th soldiers serving with the 65th Training Regiment, Sergeants Vic Colborne and Pete Baker with Trooper Clancy, drove the Royal Marine Commandos in amphibious vehicles ashore at Port Said. At the same time, the Soviet Army ruthlessly suppressed a popular uprising in Hungary. Both events created an international crisis, reservists were recalled, and on guard mounting parades, at least twelve different cap badges could be seen. Christmas leave was cancelled, and the tanks were 'bombed up' with live ammunition. Fortunately, the political situation calmed down.

In May 1957, Colonel Bob Stephen, whose father had commanded the *14th Hussars* in the First World War, became Colonel of the Regiment. In July, the Regiment moved to Hohne, close to the infamous Belsen concentration camp. In October, it reorganised: 'B' Squadron

Left: Lord Mountbatten and Major Bob English speaking to Sergeant 'Nifty' Coles, who was born in married quarters in 1908. His father, a 20th Hussar, was known as 'Busby' since he always needed a hair-cut. 'Nifty' Coles had 38 years service

Right: The officers in 1961. Back row left to right: 2/Lt Dowling, REME, 2/Lt Hodson, Lt Harman, Lt Cornish, Lt Workman, Capt de Beaujeu, 2/Lt Lee, Lt Hall, Lt Chappell, Capt Lambert. Middle row: Capt Moore, Capt Fettis, REME, The Rev Gilbert, Capt Park, Capt Pemberton, Capt Tubbs, Capt Langdon-Mudge RAPC, Capt Munro RAMC, Lt Boulter. Front row: Capt Goodhart, Maj Harris, Maj Garbutt, Maj Heath, Lt-Col Walsh, Maj Urban-Smith, Maj English, Capt Ross, Capt Pharo-Tomlin (Norwyn Photographics)

Below left: The Regimental Band, under Bandmaster Ronald Mott, in front of the Brandenburg Gate, Berlin, in 1960, before the Wall was built

deployed to Smuts Barracks, Berlin alongside Spandau Prison where Rudolf Hess and other prominent Nazis were held, 'A' and 'C' Squadrons reverted to the Armoured Personnel Carrier (APC) role, and went to Detmold and Celle. 'B' Squadron probably had more fun. As the city was under the Four-Power military occupation, all ranks were considered to be on active service. Access to East Berlin was allowed, but sometimes soldiers stayed there too long. 'B' Squadron Leader, Major Bob English, had to tell one corporal's wife that her husband had disappeared in the East; as she was cooking lunch, she quickly took one chop out of the pan, saying 'that's all right, so long as I know where he is'. Fortunately he returned safe and sound.

On 1 February 1959, Lieutenant-Colonel Ted Walsh assumed command. Although he had served as a squadron leader and second-in-command, his was the first appointment since the First World War of a commanding officer who had not been first commissioned into the *14th/20th*. His tenure proved this to be no disadvantage. A Cambridge graduate, he transferred from the Indian Cavalry after the war. He was a meticulous trainer, an excellent rifle shot and a talented artist who designed the Regimental splayed-wings vehicle emblems. He did not suffer fools gladly. On assuming command, he single-mindedly set about ensuring that the Regiment achieved the highest standards, despite being widely dispersed. In November 1960, he re-formed it at Hohne, equipped with Centurion and Conqueror tanks.

During the hectic pace of life in BAOR, troop training, live firing and exercises had to compete with exams, sport, and leave. After six months in the new role, preparations were made to receive the first Guidon since 1834. Drills were held daily, many conducted by the Colonel. On one such parade, he congratulated the rank and file on their bearing, but said that, apart from Captain Andrew Pemberton, the officers' drill was poor; the former has still to recover from the shock. At the Dress Rehearsal, to his complete surprise, Walsh was awarded the Regimental Medal by Colonel Stephen. On 10 June 1961, Field Marshal Sir Gerald Templer presented the Guidon, on behalf of The Queen, and made a most inspiring speech. Colonel

Walsh uniquely painted a picture of this Parade himself, and this now hangs in the Sergeants' Mess.

In July 1961, Lieutenant-Colonel Dickie Talbot, the veteran Reconnaissance Troop Leader and Adjutant during the war, assumed command. On 13 August, the East Germans started building the Wall to surround West Berlin. The 11th Infantry Brigade was warned for an operational advance, along the autobahn, to reinforce the Berlin Garrison. The 1st Cameronians Battle Group, with 'C' Squadron under command, was nominated for this task. Unfortunately, many officers were on leave, including the Brigade Commander, and 'C' Squadron Leader, Major Bill Garbutt. The squadron second-in-command, Captain Alan Park, who had only recently returned to regimental duty, after three years at Cambridge, was told to lead 'C' Squadron into action. This order was questioned by Major Bob English, who had been in Berlin with 'B' Squadron, and feared that the GOC Berlin, Major-General 'Jumbo' Delacombe, would be unhappy, saying the immortal words: 'Jumbo will want a field officer', i.e., himself. The plan, with or without a field officer, was fortunately not implemented, since the consequences could have been catastrophic, but the political situation remained tense, and six National Service soldiers, due for release, had their service compulsorily extended for a further six months.

While at Hohne, the *14th/20th* took over the Wessex Hounds, and Major English became Master. He hunted hounds over drag-lines around Schwarmstedt on the river Aller and to the north at Bohme, near Fallingbostel. A regimental cook, Private Fred Dibnah, helped build the kennels, and an entry in the Regimental Journal reads:

> "The new kennels were built by officers' fatigue parties, and a very good job they made of them. They were given very able and professional advice, plus some part time help, from Pte Dibnah (A.C.C.). In civilian life Dibnah is a steeplejack and still does not understand how he became a member of the A.C.C. or for that matter, the 'hound mob'."

Fred Dibnah is now a well-known television personality and presenter. Tragically, Major English was killed while training the following year and Captain Jasper Tubbs became Master. In 1962, the first Home Headquarters was established at Lancaster House, Norton Street, Manchester, alongside the Regimental Headquarters of *The Duke of Lancaster's Own Yeomanry*. The Regimental Secretary was Major Michael Urban-Smith, who

Left: Colonel Bob Stephen presenting the Regimental Medal to Lieutenant-Colonel Ted Walsh during the dress rehearsal of the 1961 Guidon Parade, to the latter's complete surprise

Below left: Lieutenant-Colonel Dickie Talbot, Commanding Officer in 1961, as a captain in 1945; his Mention in Despatches was awarded at Gilan in 1941 and worn on his tunic before the Victory Medal was issued

Below: 'C' Squadron patrolling in Cyprus after an emergency move there on Boxing Day in 1963, by John King (Steve Day; courtesy The King's Royal Hussars)

had won the MC with 43rd Reconnaissance Regiment in the war, and retired from the Army to take up the post.

In July 1962, the Regiment staged at Tidworth for two months before returning to Libya as an armoured reconnaissance regiment, after only seven years away. RHQ, 'A', 'C' and 'HQ' Squadrons went to Benghazi. 'B' Squadron went to Tripoli, where the Area Commander was Brigadier Bob Rumsey of the Royal Tank Regiment; in 1938, as a captain, Rumsey had mechanised the Regiment in India. Shortly after arrival in Libya, the most serious Cold War confrontation between the USA and the USSR took place: the Cuban missile crisis. Thanks to the statesmanship of President Kennedy, it was solved to the satisfaction of the West. While the Regiment was well away from the area of conflict, it was closely followed by everyone in Tripoli and Benghazi, on their primitive short-wave radios. The following year, the air troop, under Captain Henry Joynson, flew its first Auster aircraft into Wavell Barracks. Another pilot was Lieutenant Christopher Cornish, who was to die with Corporal N. W. Kirkham and Trooper B. L. Bunn climbing Mount Kenya two years later.

On 22 November 1963, Ramnuggur Day, the officers were holding a dinner night in the Mess at Newmarket House, and the principal guest was the US Consul-General. During dinner, he was called to the telephone only to return, ashen faced, saying: 'Colonel, my President has been shot,' to which the Colonel was heard to reply: 'Dear me, nothing too serious I hope?' At 0500 on Boxing Day, 'C' Squadron was ordered to move to Cyprus where inter-communal violence had flared up between the Greeks and Turks, and was on the island within two days. It joined a truce force with the Gloucestershire Regiment, the Rifle Brigade and the RAF Regiment, with which it worked or patrolled independently. Major Bill Garbutt led 'C' Squadron with the same dynamism as his distinguished predecessor, 'Bodge' Browne. Several troops came close to opening fire but were able to separate the two factions without doing so. Disappointingly, after only five weeks, the Squadron was recalled to Benghazi because disturbances in Libya were threatened.

In July 1964, Lieutenant-Colonel Simon Frazer took over command. Frazer came from the 15th/19th Hussars and did the opposite to his father, who had joined the *14th/20th* as a subaltern and then commanded the 15th/19th. In April 1965, Major Robin Harris took 'A' Squadron to join the United Nations Peacekeeping Force in Cyprus. Harris was an experienced operational soldier and had won the MC leading a troop in the Aden Protectorate Levies from 1957 to 1960 where he personally took part in every action and reconnaissance in the theatre at the time. In Cyprus, the Squadron patrolled the whole island, and at one time had two platoons from 2nd Grenadier Guards under command, to guard a Turkish enclave at the Lefka copper mines. This tour was the highlight of 'A' Squadron's time in the Near East for which Harris was awarded the MBE.

In early 1966, the Regiment returned home to Tidworth, and trooped the Guidon to celebrate the 250th Anniversary of the founding of the Regiment. Early in 1967, the *14th/20th* moved to Barker Barracks in Paderborn, taking over from the 13th/18th Hussars, their comrades in arms in the 'Ragged Brigade' during the Peninsular War. On arrival, Lieutenant-Colonel Peter Cavendish, from the Queen's Own Hussars, assumed command. A kinsman of the Duke of Devonshire, he proved to be one of the most effective commanding officers since the war. Despite the Duke describing the Cavendish family as 'dim', in a recent television programme, no one found such evidence in his cousin. Under his leadership, a high standard of operational readiness was achieved, against the ever present Soviet threat in the Cold

GUARDIAN OF THE PEACE

THE uneasy peace in Cyprus continues . . . kept by men like Major Bill Garbutt, aged 39, Squadron Commander of the 14/20 Hussars. Major Garbutt was making a midnight patrol in search of arms being landed along the coast.

Left: *Local newspaper report about 'C' Squadron in Cyprus (Steve Day; courtesy The King's Royal Hussars)*

Below left: *Left to right: Staff-Sergeant Charlie Osborne, Corporal Don Davies and RSM Terry Cripps outside the Guard Room at Wavell Barracks, Benghazi, in 1964*

Right: *Lieutenant Gavin Pike and Corporal Welch with Recce Troop patrolling the Inner German Border in 1967*

Below: *Captain (QGO) Amarbahardur Gurung, 2/6 GR, presenting a ceremonial kukri to Lieutenant-Colonel Simon Frazer at Benghazi*

Below right: *Lieutenant-Colonel Peter Cavendish (left) with Lieutenant-Colonel John Acland, Scots Guards, in the Libyan desert*

Above: *Princess Anne with Lieutenant-Colonel Michael Palmer and Sergeant Robin Holland on a Chieftain tank*

Left: *The Princess dining with the officers for the first time in 1969. Colonel Basil Woodd is on her left, Lieutenant-Colonel Michael Palmer is on her right and Staff Sergeant Powell, the Mess Sergeant-Major, is standing at the back (Steve Day)*

Above: Princess Anne inspecting her escort, under command of Lieutenant Michael Hill, at Government House in Hong Kong in 1971. Her equerry is Lieutenant John Symons

Above right: The Lord Mayor of Manchester, Councillor Douglas Edwards, speaking to Sergeant Lew Yankey during a recruiting tour. (His brother, Louis Edwards, was Chairman of Manchester United Football Club at the time, and served in the Regiment during the Second World War)

War, which manifested itself during the Communist invasion of Czechoslovakia in August 1968.

Having been without a royal patron since 1837, the Regiment sounded out the possibility of a Colonel-in-Chief being appointed. In 1969, the Regiment had acquired a substantial reputation under Cavendish and converted to Chieftain tanks. While training in Libya, before Gaddafi came to power, it was announced that the Queen had approved the appointment of Princess Anne as Colonel-in-Chief with effect from 1 July 1969; this followed the tradition started by Princess Frederica and King William IV.

In the Queen's Birthday Honours, Lieutenant-Colonel Peter Cavendish was awarded the OBE and Corporal Ian Rumble REME the BEM. On return to BAOR, Cavendish was promoted to full Colonel, awarded the Regimental Medal and succeeded by Lieutenant-Colonel Michael Palmer. The latter joined the *14th/20th* because his father, Lieutenant-Colonel Bobby Palmer, had commanded the *Duke of Lancaster's Own Yeomanry* at Medicina. This was particularly happy for the Regiment as he proved to be an encouraging and straightforward commanding officer to serve under, in not always easy times. In October, Princess Anne visited the Regiment in Paderborn. While dining with the officers, during her stay, Palmer presented the Princess with a personalised number plate '1420 H' for her Reliant Scimitar car. This was the brainchild of Major Christopher Ross, the second-in-command, who had obtained it from the Express Dairies in Ealing.

In September 1970, the Regiment was once more dispersed in the armoured car role: 'A' Squadron to Singapore, 'B' to Hong Kong and the remainder to Tidworth. In November 1970, 'C' Squadron carried out an operational tour in Northern Ireland, the first of many by the Regiment, which will be covered in the next chapter. In 1971, 'A' Squadron returned from Hong Kong, moved to Ulster in June, followed by RHQ and 'C' Squadron two months later.

In October, Princess Anne visited 'B' Squadron in Hong Kong, and on 17 January 1972, Lieutenant-Colonel Tom Williams, formerly of the Queen's Royal Irish Hussars,

took over command in Tidworth. There, in May, the Regiment celebrated the fiftieth anniversary of the formation of the *14th/20th King's Hussars* and Colonel Forty Allen became Colonel of the Regiment. The highlight of the year was the Shooting Team winning the King's Royal Rifle Corps Cup, the Army Major Units' Championship, which no cavalry regiment had won before. On hearing the result, a senior infantry general said: 'the infantry should hang their heads in shame'. The triumph was largely made possible by the leadership and coaching of Captain Bill Williams.

In July 1972, 'A' and 'C' Squadrons carried out further tours in Ulster, and the following year the Regiment left for Herford in Germany. 'B' Squadron, on return from Hong Kong, began a four-months' tour in Northern Ireland in October 1973, and were relieved by 'A' Squadron in February 1974. In July, Lieutenant-Colonel Bill Stockton, previously from the Royal Scots Greys, assumed command after a continuous period of regimental duty as 'B' Squadron Leader and then second-in-command. 'A' Squadron, under Major John Clifton-Bligh, was sent to the Sovereign Base Area in Cyprus in June 1975. 'C' Squadron, under Major Peter Harman, deployed to Nicosia as part of the United Nations' Force in September; on arrival, the Commander of the British Contingent, a Parachute Regiment officer, told Harman that he had no time for the Cavalry. However, at the end of their tour, this same officer was good enough to say that 'C' Squadron's performance and professionalism was way beyond what he would have expected from a unit of his own regiment.

In 1976 the *14th/20th* returned to the training role again: 'A' Squadron went to the School of Infantry and the remainder to the RAC Centre. In January 1977, Lieutenant-Colonel Stockton, a strong disciplinarian, also known as 'Hanging Bill', was awarded the OBE after his period in command, and handed over to Lieutenant-Colonel John Pharo-Tomlin at Bovington. In August Brigadier Peter Cavendish was appointed Colonel of the Regiment, and in October the Regiment returned to

Above left: Winners of the Major Units' Championship (KRRC Cup) at Bisley in 1972. Left to right, back row: Cpl Farrell, Tpr Smethurst, L/Cpl Nettleship, Tpr Holden, Sgt Marsh REME, L/Cpl Geraghty. Front row: Cpl Ingham, 2/Lt Ross, Capt Williams, Lt Col Williams, Capt Hodson, Sgt Underwood, REME (Steve Day)

Above: The Lord Mayor of Manchester, Councillor F. J. Balcombe, stirring a Christmas pudding at Herford with Lieutenant-Colonel Bill Stockton in 1974

Above: Winners of the Inter-Regimental Polo Cup in 1978, last won in 1907. Left to right: Lieutenant-Colonel John Pharo-Tomlin, Colonel Forty Allen, coach, Captain Michael Vickery, Lieutenant Anthony Woodd, Captain David Woodd, Captain Rory Mann, Trooper Abbas and Mrs Caroline Mann. Painting by Ruth Gibbons (Steve Day; courtesy The King's Royal Hussars)

Right: Lieutenant-Colonel Dan de Beaujeu leaving command in the Regiment's balloon, flown by Captain Jim Howard

Hohne, which it had left in 1962, as an armoured regiment equipped with 66 Chieftain Tanks, more than it had ever had before.

In 1978, after working up in the armoured role, infantry training started before an operational tour in Belfast; the first time the *14th/20th King's Hussars* would go on operations as a complete regiment, since 1945. At the same time, the Inter-Regimental Polo Cup, which had evaded the Regiment's grasp since 1907, was won 6–2 against the Queen's Royal Irish Hussars; Colonel Forty Allen coached the team. This success was repeated seven more times. During this period the United Services' Cup (UK v. BAOR) was won four times and the Captains' and Subalterns' Polo Cup was won five times.

In June 1979, Princess Anne inspected the whole Regiment formed up as a Battle Group with all its tanks and supporting arms. In July, Lieutenant-Colonel Dan de Beaujeu took over command. Unusually for a British

cavalry officer, he had trained at Dartmouth and his blood was French or Belgian. He joined the Army at Caterham, and was referred to as 'Guardsman de Beaujeu'; none of this affected his ability to take the Regiment to Suffield in Canada for its first ever period of training there.

In 1980, all tanks were converted to the Improved Fire Control System (IFCS). This enormous technological advance was essential for the Chieftain main armament to meet the increasing threat from Soviet tanks. In February 1981, Major-General Peter Cavendish handed over as Colonel of the Regiment to Major-General Michael Palmer, repeating history as they had done as commanding officers twelve years before. Both officers had recently been promoted, Cavendish to the International Military Staff at NATO and Palmer as Director of the Royal Armoured Corps. To have two generals serving at the same time was an unfamiliar experience for the *14th/20th*, all the more so since Major-General Palmer was the first officer commissioned into the Regiment to achieve that rank since Henry Doherty was promoted to Major-General in 1863.

In January 1982, Lieutenant-Colonel Peter Harman took over command, one of the most experienced regimental officers to do so. At the same time, Major (QM) Bill Williams, who had had an exceptional career after joining as a trooper in 1950, retired. Williams was commissioned early so did not become Regimental-Sergeant-Major, and was awarded the MBE in 1979. He generously retired to assume the post of Regimental Secretary, although this denied him the near certainty of promotion to Quartermaster Lieutenant-Colonel. Once in post, he moved Home Headquarters to Fulwood Barracks in Preston.

In June 1982, Princess Anne presented the *14th/20th King's Hussars* with their second Guidon on the same parade ground at Hohne where Field Marshal Templer

Above: Officers Uniforms worn during the Cold War, a painting presented to the Regiment by Lieutenant-Colonel Christopher Ross. The uniforms are, from left to right: mess kit, blue patrols, barrack dress, battle dress in the 3rd Infantry Division, service dress and Middle East barrack dress. (Steve Day; courtesy The King's Royal Hussars)

Above right: Princess Anne presenting the new Guidon at Hohne in 1982, painted by T. S. La Fontaine. Schloss Bredebeck, the Officers' Mess, is allegorically shown behind the parade. Left to right: Major Gordon Mitchell (1),

WO2 Butcher (2), Major-General Michael Palmer (3), HRH (4), The Chaplain General (5), Lieutenant-Colonel Peter Harman (6), Captain Alastair Wicks (7) and Colonel The Rev 'Freckles' Tilney (8). Mounted: Major David Woodd (9) and Corporal Watton (10) (Steve Day; courtesy The King's Royal Hussars)

Right: Lieutenant-Colonel John Smales with his driver, Lance-Corporal Mick Roe

had presented the first in 1961. In July 1984, Lieutenant-Colonel John Smales took over command. As a subaltern, Smales had been the victim of a medical muddle. After contracting encephalitis in Benghazi, he was evacuated to the UK. When the aircraft carrying him and one other patient suffering from paranoid psychosis landed in Malta, the medical authorities confused the two. Smales found himself locked in a room with no handle on the door and the furniture screwed to the floor, while the other patient was allowed to make his own way to hospital, carrying a bottle of vodka. Fortunately the mix-up had little effect on his career; he commanded the Regiment with wit and success, and in due course became a brigadier. In March 1985, Major-General Michael Palmer was appointed a Knight Commander of the Royal Victorian Order by the Queen, and later received a Bar to his Regimental Medal. In May, 'B' Squadron returned to Berlin after 23 years, and the rest of the Regiment went to Catterick, back in the training role for the third time since the war. In September, Reconnaissance Troop went on a six-months' operational tour to Belize, followed by a second troop in March 1986 the following year.

In January 1987, Lieutenant-Colonel Christopher Price, from the 4th/7th Royal Dragoon Guards, assumed command, the fifth Carthusian to do so. In June Princess Anne was declared Princess Royal and the following year opened the new Regimental Museum at The Old Sessions House in Preston. That year the *14th/20th* left Catterick for Münster and converted

Above: *Lieutenant-Colonel Christopher Price presenting the Regimental medal to SSM Ken Davies, who became Regimental Sergeant-Major in 1987. As a captain, Davies commanded the AI Echelon during the Gulf War and in 1992 he became Lieutenant-Colonel Quartermaster (Technical) at Bovington*

to Challenger Tanks. Also in 1987, at the instigation of the Salters' Company, one of the twelve great Livery Companies in the City of London, an association between the Regiment and the Company was formed. Many officers of the *14th/20th* were liverymen, and, at the time of the association, Mr Nicholas Hicks, a National Service officer in 'B' Squadron in 1954, was Master; Sir Michael Palmer became Master two years later.

On 9 November 1989, the local inhabitants started to demolish sections of the Berlin Wall, which the Communist authorities did little to stop. As the Soviet Army was still all-powerful, it was not apparent that this would lead to the ending of the Cold War, nor how critically it would affect the Regiment. After Lieutenant-Colonel Michael Vickery assumed command, he wrote in the Regimental Journal that he looked forward to a happy tour in Münster. While his hopes were undoubtedly fulfilled, there was to be more to it than that.

In July 1990, the Soviet threat having been greatly reduced, it was announced in Parliament that the Royal Armoured Corps would be cut from 20 regiments to twelve. Amalgamation was inevitable, and preliminary discussions were held with the 15th/19th The King's Royal Hussars, but were curtailed because of the situation in the Gulf. That month, 'B' Squadron went to the Maze in Northern Ireland as the Prison Guard Force (PGF). On 9 November, the Bishop of Blackburn dedicated the *14th/20th King's Hussars' Chapel* in Saint Lawrence Church, Barton, and consecrated the graveyard. The PGF returned in November, and in December the Regiment deployed to Saudi Arabia.

Opposite page, bottom: The interior of the Regimental Museum at Stanley Street, Preston (Norwyn Photographics)

Below: The last Colonels of the 14th/20th King's Hussars – Major-General P. B. Cavendish, CB, OBE, DL, by Robert Priseman; and Major-General Sir Michael Palmer, KCVO, by Margaret Boden (Steve Day; courtesy The King's Royal Hussars)

13 NORTHERN IRELAND

In August 1969 British troops were deployed on the streets of Belfast and London-derry, at first to keep inter-communal rioters apart. The Garrison initially provided these troops, but when the disorders intensified the Royal Ulster Constabulary required extra support. By the middle of the following year, fifteen battalions were deployed in the Province, and the Ulster Defence Regiment had been raised. On 8 November 1970, 'C' Squadron, under Major Peter Harman, arrived at Aldergrove Airport for the first tour in the Province to be carried out by the *14th/20th King's Hussars.*

'C' Squadron was in 39 Infantry Brigade, commanded by the redoubtable Brigadier Frank Kitson. Their operations involved intelligence gathering over five counties, and they also deployed several troops in Belfast at night. However as the presence of armoured cars encouraged opposition, they concentrated on patrolling with the RUC in the countryside, manning road-blocks and conducting arms searches; they even managed some useful arrests. In January 1971, the Squadron helped contain a week's trouble in Ballymurphy, and promoted good community relations. Each night, the REME Fitters Troop, under Staff Sergeant Ian Rumble, was positioned just outside the city to recover scout cars if necessary. The final four weeks were the most stimulating, with troops back in Belfast, moving at immediate notice in support of infantry battalions throughout the City. Sadly, Sergeant Platt was killed in a vehicle accident in February, but the Squadron left for Tidworth on 10 March, after a successful first tour.

Right: 'C' Squadron Leader, Major Peter Harman, briefs his second-in-command, Captain Bill Williams, on the patrol programme in the west of the province around Lough Erne, only a few miles from where the 20th Inniskilling Light Dragoons were founded in 1759

Right: Corporal
Curtis and Lance-
Corporal Parkinson
manning a 'C'
Squadron armoured
car by Holy Cross
Church in the
Crumlin Road, after
a bombing incident
(Catherine Leroy /
Sipa; Steve Day;
courtesy *TIME*
magazine)

On 9 June 1971, two months after returning from Singapore, 'A' Squadron, under Major Bill Bowles, was deployed to Gosford Castle, a Victorian folly, near Market Hill in County Armagh. Their main tasks were searches and escort duties. Following the introduction of internment, RHQ and 'C' Squadron were recalled from summer block leave to reinforce the security forces. On 10 August, RHQ moved to Bessbrook RUC Station, and Colonel Michael Palmer slept in a police cell for the first time in his life. 'C' Squadron was based in the local primary school before moving to Gosford Castle, with 'A' Squadron, which was more secure.

On 16 August, while patrolling near the Border, Corporal Peter Webb, in 'C' Squadron, approached the Customs Post at Cullaville, when his Ferret Scout car was hit by a Claymore mine and simultaneously came under automatic fire. Despite having a half-inch bolt in his jaw, he coolly returned fire before reversing out of trouble. He was subsequently awarded the MM for bravery during this incident. On 29 August 1971, another patrol, commanded by Sergeant Tottman, was ambushed near Crossmaglen. Corporal Armstrong, who was commanding the leading scout car, was killed and his driver, Trooper Ager, was seriously wounded. A Saracen APC, with Corporals McVay and Elsdon, came to rescue the injured, and after 45 minutes, although under continuous terrorist fire, Tottman extricated the patrol. Tottman was awarded a Mention in Dispatches for this action, and Corporals McVay and Elsdon, General Officer Commanding's (GOC) Commendations. By the middle of October, the entire regimental contingent had returned to Tidworth.

On 30 January 1972, paratroopers shot thirteen demonstrators dead in Londonderry. This serious over-reaction was to become known as 'Bloody Sunday', and inevitably attracted recruits to the IRA. The situation in the Province continued to deteriorate, and after Direct Rule was imposed from London on 24 March, it became clear that the Army was in for a long haul.

On 3 July, 'A' Squadron, under Major John Eyre, returned to Northern Ireland, and after the cease-fire broke, moved down to Belfast. While patrolling along the Glen Road in the Lenadoon area, Second-Lieutenant Robert Williams-Wynn was shot dead by a sniper. His driver, Trooper Brian Hansell, was wounded in the shoulder but called for support over the radio, freed the turret hatch and drove to the Musgrave Park Hospital. He was awarded a Mention in Dispatches in recognition of his bravery. 'A' Squadron later established itself in Albert Street Mill, where they supported the infantry battalions clearing 'no-go' areas during Operation 'Motorman'.

Top: 'A' Squadron Assault Troop mans a Vehicle Check Point (VCP) in 1971

Above: Sergeant Tottman with an RUC Constable in South Armagh in the summer of 1971

Left: SSM Brian Stocker, SSM Jim Howard and Sgt Ian Rumble, REME, at Aldergrove in 1973 (Lancashire Evening Post)

Right: Second-Lieutenant Robert Williams-Wynn, killed in Andersonstown in 1972. Painting by T. S. La Fontaine (Steve Day)

Below: Gosford Castle in 1974 by Ken Howard, ARA. 'A' Squadron Leader, Major Andrew Pemberton, is in the Ops Room (Steve Day)

During the last month of the tour, the Squadron was spread across the Province, SHQ being split between Londonderry and Belfast.

On 12 July, 'C' Squadron, under Major John Rawlins, moved to RAF Aldergrove for an uneventful four-months' tour, and fortunately, without casualties. Both squadrons returned in November, 'A' Squadron via Manchester where they visited 'The Hussar' pub at Hulme with the Lord Mayor. In October 1973, 'B' Squadron, under Major David Coombes, carried out the next tour, two months after its arrival in BAOR from Hong Kong. The Squadron was based at Gosford Castle under command of first, the 1st Battalion Light Infantry and then the Welsh Guards. In Newtownhamilton, the situation became lively when, following a shooting incident, a bomb injured three firemen and the squadron intelligence officer, Captain William Edge. Two car bombs followed this incident causing considerable devastation to two streets and the police station. Shortly afterwards, a 300-pound culvert bomb, south of the town, was made safe in a controlled explosion by the Ammunition Technical Officer (ATO), guarded by a troop. Staff-Sergeant Brian Draper, the Senior Non-Commissioned-Officer at the post, was 'Mentioned in Despatches' for his conduct during this period.

In February 1974, 'B' Squadron handed over to 'A' Squadron, under Major Andrew Pemberton, with troops at Newcastle, Newry and Newtownhamilton. The 1st Troop, under Lieutenant David Bowes-Lyon, arrested a total of nineteen suspected terrorists, found three weapons and 90 pounds of explosives. The 3rd Troop, under Second-Lieutenant Colin Wetherall-Pepper, surprised three terrorist bombers and chased them under fire across the Border. Two were captured and made to defuse the bomb in their truck; they were later sentenced to five years' imprisonment. Wetherell-Pepper was subsequently awarded a Mention in Dispatches. During the tour, very sadly, Corporal Michael Herbert, Corporal Michael Cotton and Trooper John Tyson were killed while on duty. 'A' Squadron returned to Herford in June, and there were to be no further Ulster tours for four years.

In July 1978, the Regiment, under Lieutenant-Colonel John Pharo-Tomlin, was dismounted and carried out three months' training in preparation for taking over the Andersonstown, Lenadoon and Twinbrook areas of West Belfast, from the 1st Queen's Regiment. This was a hard republican area with an equally hard loyalist enclave, and the *14th/20th* was the first non infantry regiment to have responsibility for that Tactical Area of Responsibility (TAOR). The CO of 3rd Parachute Regiment, predecessors to 1 QUEENS, said that he held up his hands in horror when he heard that 'his' TAOR was to be patrolled by a cavalry regiment. As the Regiment had never operated exclusively in the infantry role, it was necessary for the three months' preparatory training to be very thorough, to ensure that operational tasks were carried out effectively and casualties avoided. On 10 November, the Regiment moved to Belfast in RAF Hercules aircraft. 'A' Squadron, under Major John Smales, and 'B' Squadron, under Major Kerry Hodson, the only Irish squadron leader, were based in Woodburn RUC Station. 'D' Squadron, under Major David Coombes, and the Close Observation Troop, under Captain Roger Fellowes, were at Glassmullin Camp. Tac HQ, where Major William Edge was operations officer, was at Fort Monagh, the most mortared camp in Belfast, and shared the base with No 1 Company 1st Coldstream Guards. The Echelon (Administration) was at Musgrave Park Hospital, under the Quartermaster Major Eddy Sheen, a location sometimes unkindly known as 'Sleepy Hollow'.

Right: The Rover Group at Fort Monagh in 1979. Left to right: Corporal 'Mac' McNally, Lieutenant-Colonel John Pharo-Tomlin and Lance-Corporal Dave Bache

Below right: Brigadier David Ramsbotham, Commander of 39 Infantry Brigade (left), with Major Kerry Hodson, 'B' Squadron Leader, in his TAOR at Twinbrook

On arrival, it was vital to show the opposition that the *14th/20th* were up to the job and as fighting fit as 1 QUEENS, a first-class battalion with high morale. As many soldiers had lost their lives in the TAOR, before and since, including Second-Lieutenant Williams-Wynn in 1972, patrolling started fairly aggressively, but great store was also set on fostering good relations with the local population. The Roman Catholic Community Relations Officer, Major Michael Cullinan, met so many priests that he tended to forget where he was; one morning when receiving orders from the commanding officer, he called him 'Father'. The pattern of patrolling was in four-man 'bricks', often in company with the RUC, who now had primacy. While the tour may not have had some of the excitements as during the time of Operation 'Motorman', there were enough criminals around to keep everyone busy. Principal threats were bombs and snipers, which fortunately did not connect with the *14th/20th*, though one morning an unfortunate guardsman was shot in the heel by an AK 47, while driving into Fort Monagh. The Regiment made some good finds of arms, ammunition and explosives, and also some good arrests.

The Regiment was fortunate to serve under two exceptional Commanders of 39 Infantry Brigade, Brigadiers John Macmillan and David Ramsbotham. The latter was Chief Inspector of Prisons until recently. When the tour ended, the GOC, Lieutenant-General Sir Timothy Creasey, signalled: 'I send all of you my warmest congratulations and thanks for your hard work during a most successful tour. Well done!' While it was gratifying to receive this praise, the greatest comfort was to return to Germany without having incurred any casualties, and having inflicted none on the populace in West Belfast. The *14th/20th* had performed professionally in an unfamiliar role, and in recognition of this Lieutenant Richard Shirreff and Sergeant Geoff Hutchinson were awarded GOC's Commendations, and the

Left: *Lieutenant Richard Shirreff and his troop patrolling Twinbrook in 1979, by Joseph McWilliams* (Steve Day; courtesy The King's Royal Hussars)

Commanding Officer, Lieutenant-Colonel John Pharo-Tomlin was 'Mentioned in Dispatches'.

There were to be no further Ulster tours for more than ten years, but terrorist activity occurred in Germany. On 1 September 1989, Troopers Steven Costello and Howard Pickering were shot while off duty in Münster. Both sustained serious gunshot wounds and were admitted to the British Military Hospital in Münster.

On 17 April 1990, 'B' Squadron, reinforced by other squadrons, began three months' dismounted training, prior to taking over as the Prison Guard Force (PGF) at the Maze Prison. 0n 20 July the Squadron, under Major Richard Shirreff, was fully operational for the last emergency tour in Northern Ireland to be carried out by the *14th/20th King's Hussars.* They operated in three troop cycles of five days: Defence, to defend the Maze from external attack by manning the watch towers; Ground Defence Area (GDA), providing rural patrols around the prison; and Quick Reaction Forces (QRFs), Lisburn patrols, under command of the Royal Military Police, manning vehicle check points and foot patrols to prevent terrorists from West Belfast attacking inviting military targets in the area.

A fourth and most interesting task was providing a small reserve for 39 Infantry Brigade for operations in South Down and in such areas in Belfast as the Lower Falls, Divis Flats, Ardoyne or Ballymurphy. In the Springfield Road, Corporal McAleese and his team were the first soldiers in the *14th/20th* to come under fire since the 1970s. Unfortunately, as they were unable to identify the firing point, they could not return fire. The other contact was by Corporal Dickinson and his team, which was on the receiving end of an improvised anti-armour grenade in New Barnsley. Luckily this dangerous device failed to explode, as the thrower's primary intention appeared to be on making a rapid escape. Other teams also had interesting confrontations, from various missiles thrown with habitual accuracy.

'B' Squadron left the Province on 20 October 1990, after a successful tour, for block leave. It rejoined the Regiment in Münster on 12 November and moved to Saudi Arabia a month later.

14 THE GULF WAR

On 2 August 1990, Iraqi troops invaded Kuwait, which posed a threat to both the stability of the region and Western oil supplies. As it also looked as if Saudi Arabia could well be Saddam Hussein's next target, President George Bush (Senior) managed to get a coalition of allied forces together. The British contribution was initially from the Royal Navy, Royal Engineers, Royal Signals and Royal Air Force. But on 7 September it was decided to include ground troops in the form of 7th Armoured Brigade. This brigade needed reinforcement, so Captain Alistair Todd and one troop, led by Lieutenant Mike Rayner, was sent to the Royal Scots Dragoon Guards. The 7th Armoured Brigade needed a high level of spares, so *14th/20th* tanks in Münster had to be cannibalised to achieve this, leaving only one tank intact for training.

Despite the troop build-up in Saudi Arabia, it became clear that the Iraqis would not withdraw but must be evicted by force. On 22 November, it was announced that 4th Armoured Brigade, comprising: *14th/20th King's Hussars*, 1st Battalion Royal Scots, 3rd Battalion Royal Regiment of Fusiliers (RRF) and supporting arms, would also be sent. The Regiment now needed to rebuild its emasculated tank fleet, and to bring its personnel strength up to war establishment. Reinforcements came from *6th Gurkha Rifles*, 13th/18th Royal Hussars, 4th Royal Tank Regiment and, on 2 December, 'A' Squadron, The Life Guards, under Major James Hewitt. By 9 December all the vehicles of the *14th/20th* Battle Group had sailed from the port of Emden for Al

Below: Major Alastair Wicks (left), with Sergeant Brian Lythgoe, leading 'D' Squadron in the Saudi Arabian desert before the ground war began (Mike Moore / Imperial War Museum)

Jubayl, and the main body flew out to the Gulf from 20 to 27 December. By 2 January 1991, the Regiment was complete in its desert training area.

On 4 January, the GOC 1st Armoured Division, Major-General Rupert Smith, arrived to discuss the tactical battle ahead, and on the 8th the Prime Minister, John Major, visited. During the next month intensive training, including study days and field exercises at battle group, brigade and divisional level, took place. The tanks also had improved armour fitted. On 17 January, the air war began. On the 25th operational ammunition was issued, and Robert Fox, the Defence Correspondent of the *Daily Telegraph*, joined the Battle Group. On 26–28 January the Regiment moved up to the divisional concentration area KEYS, a stretch of flat featureless desert, located by the satellite navigation computer, some 200 miles to the north-west. The tanks moved on tank transporters, and the crews by Hercules, and then Chinook helicopters. The rainy season had started in earnest and, like the *14th Hussars* in Mesopotamia in 1917, the regiment got cold and wet in the desert. The closer the Regiment got to Iraq, the higher their state of readiness became, as did their concern over Saddam's biological and chemical missile potential. Nuclear, biological and chemical (NBC) training was very well attended.

Training and refining of equipment continued until 21 February when the Commanding Officer, Lieutenant-Colonel Mike Vickery, formally gave orders for the forthcoming operations. It had been 45 years since the last time the *14th/20th King's Hussars* as an armoured regiment on active service had had such orders. Those had been given by Lieutenant-Colonel 'Freckles' Tilney, the father of Vickery's Second-in-Command, Major

Top left: Recce Troop being briefed. The group includes, left to right clockwise: Troopers Duane Hesketh, Paul Buckley, Acky Green, 4RTR, Lance-Corporal Joe Pope, Lieutenant Jeremy Denning, Trooper Stu Craddock, Lance-Corporal Heath Eynon, Troopers Simon Airey and Steve Davis (Mike Moore / Imperial War Museum)

Centre left: The Prime Minister, John Major, with Lieutenant-Colonel Michael Vickery on 8 January 1991 (Norwyn Photographics)

Bottom left: The Brigade Liaison Officer, WO1, later Captain, 'JC' Cornish, who became the Assistant Regimental Secretary (North) of The King's Royal Hussars

Right: Lance Corporal Redgrave with Lieutenant-Colonel Mike Vickery bombing up the CO's tank

Godfrey Tilney. Also present to receive the Gulf War orders were Major Peter Garbutt, Captains Jonty Palmer, Alastair Ross and Andrew Gossage, sons or grandsons of former regimental officers. Reconnaissance Troop then moved north to liaise with HQ 3 (US) Brigade, and a day later Tactical Headquarters (TAC HQ) moved forward to join up with the US Brigade HQ. G-Day ('Go'-Day) was fixed for 24 February.

The *14th/20th Battle Group* moved to a staging area just south of the Iraqi border on the 25th and then led 4th Armoured Brigade north through a US-held border breach.

At 1930 it left the Forming Up Place (FUP), and started the advance to contact as the Brigade's point battle group: 'A' Squadron, under Major Peter Garbutt, left; 'B' Squadron, under Major Richard Shirreff, right; 'D' Squadron, under Major Alistair Wicks, and The Queen's Company, Grenadier Guards, under Major Grant Baker, in reserve.

The first contact was made at 2230 by 'B' Squadron who engaged a variety of enemy targets over the next hour. As resistance crumbled, the Queen's Company cleared the position and received the surrendering prisoners. The advance continued at 0315 on 26 February, and many more T55 tanks were engaged. It was later confirmed that five had been destroyed by 'B' Squadron. This action was to be known as the Battle of Al Haniyah; 'B' Squadron being now less than fully bombed-up was relieved by 'D' Squadron on the right.

'A' Squadron Leader had said in his orders on 24 February: 'Our mission is to destroy all enemy within boundaries', clear and decisive. The Squadron's first engagements came early on 26 February, mainly with machine-guns, after which it moved through its objective at 0630. Later, with 'D' Squadron on the right, the Squadron prepared for the Brigade assault on Objective BRASS. It crossed the start-line at 1010, to find, disappointingly, that most enemy tanks had already been knocked out by American aircraft, and when the objective was reached, there were only a few targets to engage. At 1930, it moved under command of the Royal Scots, before attacking an Iraqi armoured brigade on Objective TUNGSTEN. The assaults on TUNGSTEN were launched between 0230 and 0530 on 27 February, during which two troops of 'A' Squadron destroyed a company of T55 tanks. At first light the Squadron rejoined the *14th/20th* Battle Group which advanced north-east at 1330. During the move forward, and with clearance to engage, two armoured vehicles were destroyed at a range of 4,000 metres. These unfortunately turned out to be Spartans from 16 Air Defence Regiment, some four kilometres astray from their stated position. Luckily the crews were dismounted, but they suffered burns and needed medical evacuation.

Meanwhile, 'D' Squadron was in reserve until 0400 on 26 February, when it was tasked with investigating a heat source north of the Battle Group axis. In the nick of

Right: *Major Richard Shirreff, 'B' Squadron Leader, and Major Peter Garbutt, 'A' Squadron Leader wearing the traditional 20th Hussars cap badge*

Below: *An Iraqi T55 tank destroyed and on fire (Mike Moore / Imperial War Museum)*

time, this was discovered to be a Royal Signals vehicle, also in the wrong place. At 0615, after relieving 'B' Squadron on the right, they advanced to assault the enemy positions on BRASS, which were destroyed without fuss. On reaching the final objective, a tank brigade of some 50 tanks and APCs was in evidence; many vehicles had already been destroyed but those left were efficiently despatched by 'D' Squadron. After BRASS had been secured, the Squadron regrouped with 3rd RRF which involved moving back over ground already taken. It then led the 3 RRF battle group south-east on to Objective STEEL, a series of artillery positions. The main position was taken by 1500, two troops supported two RRF companies in clearing the one in depth, which was a brigade position.

While consolidating on STEEL two large explosions were heard; two American A10 anti-tank aircraft had mistakenly destroyed two RRF Warriors, killing nine soldiers and wounding eleven. At 2330, after replenishing with fuel and ammunition, 'D' Squadron moved east, joined by 'B' Squadron, on the southern half of TUNGSTEN, still under command of 3RRF. Light resistance was encountered until 0430 on 27 February when the squadrons halted. At 1400 it moved east to regroup with the *14th/20th* Battle group over the Wadi-al-Batin on the Kuwaiti border.

At 0630 on 28 February, the Regiment moved off at some speed, 'B' and 'D' Squadrons leading, with orders to advance to the north of Kuwait City, and cut off any Iraqi troops withdrawing towards Basra. Before they could reach the City, the Cease-Fire was called, and at 0825 the *14th/20th King's Hussars Battle Group* was ordered to halt in the Kuwait desert. A period of regrouping, individual training and an impromptu gunnery camp, using T-55s, followed. On 18 March, the Band, who had been Medical Orderlies during the campaign, gave an excellent concert to all ranks. Their instruments had been flown up from Al Jubayl in a C-130.

Above left: General Norman Schwarz-kopf, thanking 'D' Squadron for staying behind in Kuwait after the regiment was back in Münster (Mike Moore / Imperial War Museum)

Above: The Quartermaster and OC 'B'1 Echelon, Major, later Lieutenant-Colonel, 'Drac' Draper

Above right: Lieutenant-Colonel Mike Vickery and his 'loader', Captain Jonty Palmer, after the ceasefire (Imperial War Museum)

Right: Blazing oil wells in Kuwait (Imperial War Museum)

The Gulf War was the last campaign in the 277-year history of the *14th/20th King's Hussars*. No soldier in the Battle Group had been lost, although some injuries were sustained. They undoubtedly distinguished themselves, showing that they were highly professional tank soldiers. The Regiment was well led at all levels, well trained and morale was high. Acclaim must go to the Commanding Officer, Lieutenant-Colonel Mike Vickery, who was subsequently awarded the Order of the British Empire (OBE). Other awards were received by: Major Peter Garbutt, Mention in Dispatches; Captain Paul Jaques REME, US Bronze Star Medal; Corporal Alan Hewitt, Commander British Forces, Middle East Commendation. The *14th/20th King's Hussars* were later awarded *GULF 1991*, as a Theatre Honour, to be emblazoned on the Guidon, and *WADI AL BATIN* as a Battle Honour.

On 4 April 1991, the Main Body of the Regiment was back in Münster, followed by 'D' Squadron a month later; they had been left behind with the 3 RRF Battle Group to defend Kuwait. By mid May, after leave, the *14th/20th* were back complete and ready for the BAOR rat race once more. During the year it was announced that a further amalgamation in the Royal Armoured Corps would be necessary. The logical discussions, which had started with the 15th/19th the previous year, were discontinued after they indicated a preference to combine with the 13th/18th Hussars, a regiment from the same side of the Pennines. Further discussions within the Cavalry took place and on 23 July 1991 it was announced, by the Chief of the General Staff that *The Royal Hussars (Prince of Wales's Own)* were to amalgamate with the *14th/20th King's Hussars* to form a single armoured regiment.

On 10 June 1992, Lieutenant-Colonel David Woodd followed in his father's footsteps and assumed command of the *14th/20th King's Hussars* during a colourful handover parade with both Commanding Officers and the Adjutant mounted. On 24 August, the Regiment received the Freedom of the Borough of South Ribble, and on 6 November, the Freedom of the Borough of Preston. On 27 November 1992, the *14th/20th King's Hussars'* Regimental Flag was lowered for the last time after a poignant parade at York Barracks. This was the last day that *14th/20th* uniform was worn, and brought to an end the seventy years since the first amalgamation in 1922. While this second amalgamation was unwelcome, it is worth quoting the valedictory

Below: The officers wearing their Gulf Medals in April 1992 for the final group photograph before amalgamation in December. Left to right: back row, Captain S. T. Arrowsmith, Captain J. A. Frost, Second Lieutenant R. A. S. Macwatt, Lieutenant C. P. M. Mowat, Lieutenant J. D. Hollands, Captain M. N. Munday, Major J. R. M. Palmer, Captain S. J. M. Graham; centre row, Lieutenant M. S. Rayner, Lieutenant E. T. Gimlette, Captain D. N. S. Wood, Lieutenant J. C. Cornish, Captain R. F. Tyson, Lieutenant-Colonel J. M. D. Moger, Lieutenant-Colonel A. R. D. Shirreff, Major D. J. A. Williams, MBE, Lieutenant A. C. Harman, Captain S. R. C. Searight, Captain J. C. V. Denning, Captain R. A. U. Todd; front row,

Colonel C. K. Price, Major A. D. Gallie, Major N. G. T. Polley, Major A. F. B. Ashbrooke, Captain A. A. Gossage, Lieutenant-Colonel M. J. H. Vickery, OBE, Major-General Sir Michael Palmer, KCVO, Major T. C. Tayler, Major H. A. O. Wicks, Major J. R. C. de Normann, Major B. J. M. Draper, Colonel J. R. Clifton-Bligh, Colonel J. P. Smales (Norwyn Photographics)

remarks in the 1991 edition of the Regimental Journal, *The Hawk*, made by Lieutenant-Colonel Mike Vickery:

> "Please don't waste too much time mourning the passing of the *14th/20th King's Hussars*; we shall still be there in *The King's Royal Hussars*, and I am confident that the same spirit will prevail to make the new regiment an altogether worthy successor to its forbears."

The Amalgamation Parade was held on 4 December 1992, at York Barracks in the presence of The Princess Royal. The Colonel of the new Regiment was Major-General

Right: *Sergeant Ken Crick and Bandsman Richard Kemp at the Rhine Army Summer Show in 1992. Both were medical orderlies during the Gulf War, and Crick became a paramedic in Yorkshire after leaving the Army* (Norwyn Photographics; courtesy *Soldier* Magazine)

John Friedberger from the *Royal Hussars,* and the Commanding Officer was Lieutenant-Colonel David Woodd. Home Headquarters became *Home Headquarters (North),* Major Bill Williams remained as Regimental Secretary and was later awarded a second Bar to his Regimental Medal, shortly before he retired.

In June 2000, Her Royal Highness presented *The King's Royal Hussars* with their first Guidon, in a spectacular parade at Tidworth. During the ceremony, the old

Left: Major Bill Williams receiving the Second Bar to his Regimental Medal from Lieutenant-Colonel Adrian Bradshaw (Lancashire Evening Post)

Below: The Princess Royal at the Amalgamation Parade in Münster, on 4 December 1992, with Lieutenant-Colonel David Woodd (left), Major-General John Friedberger, Colonel of the Regiment, and Bandmaster Colin Hicks, who is on the left of HRH

Guidon of the *14th/20th King's Hussars* was marched off for the last time, which underlined the passing of the *14th/20th,* and confirmed *The King's Royal Hussars* as the successor. Since amalgamation, the new Regiment has distinguished itself in many fields, particularly on operations in Northern Ireland, Bosnia and Kosovo. *The King's Royal Hussars* are undoubtedly worthy heirs to their forebears and enjoy a reputation in the British Army second to none.

ROLL OF HONOUR

DEDICATION

IN PROUD AND GRATEFUL MEMORY
THIS ROLL OF HONOUR IS DEDICATED
TO ALL MEMBERS OF THE

14TH DRAGOONS

14TH LIGHT DRAGOONS

20TH JAMAICA LIGHT DRAGOONS

14TH (DUCHESS OF YORK'S OWN)
LIGHT DRAGOONS

20TH LIGHT DRAGOONS

14TH (THE KING'S) REGIMENT
OF LIGHT DRAGOONS

14TH (KING'S) HUSSARS

20TH HUSSARS

14TH/20TH HUSSARS

14TH/20TH KING'S HUSSARS

WHO DIED IN THE SERVICE
OF THEIR COUNTRY AND WHOSE NAMES
ARE RECORDED HEREIN
OR ARE KNOWN ONLY TO GOD

W.E W.I.L.L R.E.M.E.M.B.E.R T.H.E.M

Left: *The Roll of Honour book: far left, the cover; near left, the dedication page* [Norwyn Photographics]

The Regimental Roll of Honour lists all those killed on, or as the result of, active service since 1795. It does not include those officers and soldiers who have died, for whatever reason, when serving outside an operational theatre. It is known, however, that the early Casualty Lists for the Regiment may be incomplete. Recording of such data has been much better for the twentieth century.

Year	Surname	Initial	Rank	Regiment	Place
REVOLUTIONARY & NAPOLEONIC WARS, 1793–1815					
1795	Mc Bride		QM	20 LD	Jamaica
	Sandford	G	LtCol	20 LD	Jamaica
1805	Gunstan	J	Pte	20 LD	Jamaica
	Hester	L	Pte	20 LD	Castelmare
	Nudick	J	Pte	20 LD	Castelmare
	Thomas	M	Pte	20 LD	Messina
1806	Ansell	J	Pte	20 LD	Messina
	Batley	J	Pte	20 LD	Capetown
	Brooks	H	Sgt	20 LD	Messina
	Catterell	T	Pte	20 LD	Messina
	Combly	J	Pte	20 LD	Maldonado
	Coyle	G	Pte	20 LD	Messina
	Cross	J	Sgt	20 LD	Messina
	Davies	E	Pte	20 LD	Capetown
	Fulcher	C	Sgt	20 LD	Maldonado
	Gorres	P	Cpl	20 LD	Capetown
	Gould	T	Pte	20 LD	Capetown
	Horton	J	Pte	20 LD	Maldonado
	Horton	W	Pte	20 LD	Messina
	Jones	F	Pte	20 LD	Messina
	Kendall	M	Pte	20 LD	Messina
	Lawrence	J	Pte	20 LD	Maldonado
	Maize	B	Pte	20 LD	Maldonado

Year	Surname	Initial	Rank	Regiment	Place
1806	Moulton	S	Pte	20 LD	Capetown
	Parks	W	Pte	20 LD	Messina
	Phippen	N	Pte	20 LD	Messina
	Redfern	J	Pte	20 LD	Messina
	Roach	J	Pte	20 LD	Messina
	Sheppard	J	QM	20 LD	Capetown
	Stimpson	J	Pte	20 LD	Capetown
	Struhers	D	Pte	20 LD	Messina
	Taylor	J	Sgt	20 LD	at Sea
	Thomas	G	Pte	20 LD	Capetown
	Waters	L	Pte	20 LD	Capetown
1807	Bestick	W	Pte	20 LD	Messina
	Courtnay	G	Pte	20 LD	Messina
	Dance	A	Pte	20 LD	Monte Video
	Edwards	B	Pte	20 LD	Messina
	Farr	p	Pte	20 LD	Monte Video
	Jonk	F	Pte	20 LD	Messina
	Lancaster	T	Pte	20 LD	Monte Video
	McCorton	M	Pte	20 LD	Messina
	McKenzie	A	Sgt	20 LD	Messina
	McNeal	H	Pte	20 LD	Messina
	Parr	J	Pte	20 LD	Messina
	Saxton	R	Pte	20 LD	Messina
	Scheere	J	Pte	20 LD	Messina
	Silaz	G	Pte	20 LD	Messina

Year	Surname	Initial	Rank	Regiment	Place
1807	Waldman	H	Ptte	20 LD	Maldonado
1808	Alsop	J	Pte	20 LD	Lisbon
	Beechall	T	Pte	20 LD	Vimiera
	Beecher	J	Pte	20 LD	Belem
	Bodie	W	Pte	20 LD	Belem
	Boswell	C	Pte	20 LD	Belem
	Brady	J	Pte	20 LD	Vimiera
	Brock	J	Tptr	20 LD	Messina
	Brown	W	Pte	20 LD	at Sea
	Capps	J	Pte	20 LD	Messina
	Chilman	J	Pte	20 LD	Alcantara
	Cooke	C	Pte	20 LD	Belem
	Cosgrove	J	Pte	20 LD	Vimiera
	Glasgow	W	Pte	20 LD	Vimiera
	Harvey	J	Pte	20 LD	Vimiera
	Haxton	p	Pte	20 LD	Lisbon
	Hearbour	W	Pte	20 LD	Alcantara
	Hitzman	C	Pte	20 LD	Vimiera
	Hobble	T	Pte	20 LD	Messina
	Holmes	R	Pte	20 LD	Belem
	James	S	Pte	20 LD	Belem
	Kent	W	Cpl	20 LD	Belem
	Kinsman	J	Pte	20 LD	Alcantara
	Kottero	J	Pte	20 LD	Vimiera
	Lovett	W	Pte	20 LD	Alcantara
	Middleton	W	Pte	20 LD	Belem
	Morris	G	Pte	20 LD	Messina
	Myers	W	Pte	20 LD	at Sea
	Nicholas	W	Pte	20 LD	Belem
	Nightingale	J	Pte	20 LD	Vimiera
	Poole	J	Pte	20 LD	Belem
	Sadler	G	Pte	20 LD	Vimiera
	Shluck	A	Pte	20 LD	Alcantara
	Shorter	S	Pte	20 LD	Belem
	Simms	J	Pte	20 LD	Vimiera
	Stroud	T	Pte	20 LD	Messina
	Sullivan	P	Pte	20 LD	Messina
	Taylor	C	LtCol	20 LD	Vimiera
	Thicket	J	Pte	20 LD	Messina
	Thompson	J	Pte	20 LD	Messina
	Tribe	J	Pte	20 LD	Vimiera
	Weston	J	Pte	20 LD	Belem
	Weeks	W	Pte	20 LD	Alcantara
	Williams	J	Pte	20 LD	Vimiera
1809	Adams	J	Pte	14 LD	Belem
	Adcock	E	Pte	14 LD	Santarem
	Allen	J	Pte	14 LD	Santarem
	Ashford	J	Pte	14 LD	Santarem
	Atkinson	J	Pte	14 LD	Santarem
	Bailey	J	Pte	20 LD	Messina
	Baker	G	Ptte	14 LD	Santarem
	Bampton	R	Pte	14 LD	Villa Vicosa
	Barker	G	Pte	14 LD	Villa Vicosa
	Barnes	T	Pte	14 LD	Santarem
	Baycott	J	Pte	14 LD	Santarem
	Beasley	B	Pte	14 LD	Oporto
	Bends	A	Pte	14 LD	Villa Vicosa
	Benson	T	Pte	20 LD	Messina
	Bentley	W	Pte	14 LD	Santarem
	Bidgood	J	Pte	14 LD	Santarem
	Bisshop	J	Pte	14 LD	Villa Vicosa
	Bolton	R	QM	20 LD	Lisbon
	Bond	G	Pte	14 LD	Oporto
1809	Brabston	C	Pte	20 LD	Messina
	Browne	H	Pte	14 LD	Santarem
	Browne	T	Pte	14 LD	Villa Vicosa
	Buckley	J	Pte	14 LD	Santarem
	Bunn	J	Pte	14 LD	Santarem
	Burton	W	Pte	14 LD	Santarem
	Cadman	W	Cpl	14 LD	Villa Vicosa
	Carker	S	Pte	14 LD	Santarem
	Carress	J	Pte	14 LD	Thamar
	Chilman	J	Pte	20 LD	Messina
	Chapman	J	Pte	14 LD	Villa Vicosa
	Churchill	D	Pte	14 LD	Villa Vicosa
	Clarke	W	Pte	14 LD	Villa Vicosa
	Coates	W	Pte	14 LD	Santarem
	Connor	J	Pte	14 LD	Santarem
	Cooper	J	Pte	14 LD	Villa Vicosa
	Cope	S	Pte	14 LD	Villa Vicosa
	Cox	B	Pte	14 LD	Oporto
	Cox	J	Pte	14 LD	POW
	Cox	T	Pte	14 LD	Santarem
	Crutton	W	Pte	14 LD	Thamar
	Daley	J	Sgt	14 LD	Santarem
	Debble	T	Pte	14 LD	Santarem
	Deluce	W	Pte	14 LD	Santarem
	Dizon	W	Pte	14 LD	Santarem
	Domain	T	Pte	14 LD	Santarem
	Draper	J	Pte	20 LD	Messina
	Eades	J	Pte	14 LD	Villa Vicosa
	Eustace	A	Maj	20 LD	Abrantes
	Forest	S	Pte	20 LD	Messina
	Fox	C	Pte	14 LD	Santarem
	Gainer	B	Pte	14 LD	Santarem
	Grady	J	Pte	14 LD	Santarem
	Guifford	J	Pte	14 LD	Santarem
	Harbour	R	Pte	14 LD	Santarem
	Hart	T	Pte	20 LD	Messina
	Harrigan	P	Pte	14 LD	Oporto
	Heath	S	Pte	14 LD	Santarem
	Herd	W	Pte	14 LD	Talavera
	Hervey	W	Pte	14 LD	Villa Vicosa
	Hitchcock	J	Pte	14 LD	Santarem
	Holloway	G	Pte	14 LD	Santarem
	Hoyles	J	Pte	14 LD	Santarem
	Ivetts	J	Pte	14 LD	Santarem
	Jones	J	Pte	14 LD	Oporto
	Jones	J	Pte	14 LD	Villa Vicosa
	Jones	T	Pte	14 LD	Santarem
	Kennedy	W	Pte	20 LD	Messina
	Lane	W	Pte	14 LD	Santarem
	Lansdown	J	Pte	14 LD	Santarem
	Lawder	D	Pte	14 LD	Santarem
	Lees	J	Pte	14 LD	Santarem
	McCue	P	Pte	20 LD	Messina
	McDonaugh	D	Pte	20 LD	Messina
	Merriott	W	Pte	14 LD	Oporto
	Midwood	M	Pte	14 LD	Santarem
	Milsom	W	Cpl	14 LD	Oporto
	Moore	J	Pte	14 LD	Santarem
	Moss	J	Pte	14 LD	Villa Vicosa
	Neighbour	T	Pte	14 LD	Santarem
	Newmarch	W	Pte	14 LD	Santarem
	Nicolls	W	Pte	14 LD	Santarem
	Nixon	E	Pte	14 LD	Santarem

Year	Surname	Initial	Rank	Regiment	Place	Year	Surname	Initial	Rank	Regiment	Place
1809	Noon	W	Cpl	20 LD	Messina	1810	Cross	W	Pte	14 LD	Milheada
	Olliver	T	Pte	14 LD	Santarem		Duckworth	D	Pte	14 LD	Sobral
	O'Neally	P	Pte	14 LD	Santarem		Eades	W	Pte	14 LD	POW Talavera
	Page	J	Pte	14 LD	Santarem						
	Pitt	E	Pte	14 LD	Oporto		Ensor	T	Pte	14 LD	POW Talavera
	Price	R	Pte	14 LD	Oporto						
	Pugh	J	Pte	14 LD	Santarem		Goldstone	R	Pte	14 LD	Sexmiro
	Rance	J	Pte	14 LD	Santarem		Goodman	R	Pte	14 LD	Santarem
	Ray	J	Pte	14 LD	Santarem		Gregory	W	Pte	14 LD	Sobral
	Read	D	Pte	20 LD	Messina		Hankes	C	Pte	14 LD	Sexmiro
	Riely	P	Pte	14 LD	Santarem		Heathcock	S	Pte	14 LD	Santarem
	Robinett	T	Pte	14 LD	Santarem		Horner	G	Pte	14 LD	Sexmiro
	Saint	J	Pte	14 LD	Oporto		Hughes	A	Cpl	14 LD	Sobral
	Shelton	W	Pte	14 LD	Talavera		Hughes	J	Cpl	14 LD	Sobral
	Skillman	W	Pte	14 LD	Villa Vicosa		Jones	E	Pte	14 LD	Torres Vedras
	Smith	A	Sgt	14 LD	Santarem						
	Smith	W	Pte	20 LD	Messina		King	W	Pte	14 LD	Sexmiro
	Spooner	W	Pte	14 LD	Santarem		Kirkbright	T	Pte	14 LD	Santarem
	Stacey	W	Pte	14 LD	Villa Vicosa		Lawrence	W	Sgt	14 LD	Abrantes
	State	M	Pte	14 LD	Talavera		Lomax	R	Cpl	14 LD	Frexadas
	Stephens	T	Tptr	14 LD	Santarem		Mc Cormack		QM	14 LD	Sexmiro
	Stewart	J	Pte	14 LD	Santarem		McGowan	T	Pte	14 LD	Almeida
	Stickley	J	Pte	14 LD	Santarem		McCredie	J	Pte	14 LD	Santarem
	Taylor	J	Pte	14 LD	Talavera		Patterson	J	Sgt	14 LD	Almeida
	Till	P	Pte	14 LD	Ciudad Rodrigo		Pearce	T	Pte	14 LD	Santarem
							Robins	F	Pte	14 LD	Coimbra
	Trim	J	Pte	20 LD	Messina		Rutland	G	Pte	14 LD	POW Talavera
	Tyrer	W	Pte	20 LD	Messina						
	Vaughan	M	Pte	14 LD	Campo Mayor		Sammoy	D	Pte	14 LD	POW Talavera
	Venus	M	Pte	14 LD	Campo Mayor		Smith	T	Pte	14 LD	Santarem
							Talbot	N	LtCol	14 LD	Sexmiro
	Walshe	J	Pte	14 LD	Oporto		Tarrow	J	Pte	14 LD	Aronches
	Ware	G	Pte	14 LD	Alcantara		Topper	J	Pte	14 LD	Santarem
	Warwick	C	Pte	14 LD	Villa Vicosa		Whealy	J	Pte	14 LD	Sobral
	Webber	J	Pte	14 LD	Alcantara		Wildman	J	Pte	14 LD	Almeida
	Wheeler	W	Pte	14 LD	Oporto		Wilmot	A	Pte	14 LD	Santarem
	Wise	P	Pte	20 LD	Messina		Woods	T	Pte	14 LD	POW Talavera
	Whitworth	T	Pte	14 LD	Alcantara						
	Woods	T	Pte	14 LD	Alcantara		Wooldridge	T	Pte	14 LD	Santarem
	Wren	J	Pte	14 LD	Oporto		Young	J	Pte	14 LD	Lisbon
1810	Allen	W	Pte	14 LD	POW Talavera	1811	Adams	J	Pte	14 LD	Sobral
							Arnold	W	Pte	14 LD	Fuentes d'Onor
	Balmer	J	Pte	14 LD	Sexmiro						
	Belton	T	Pte	14 LD	Milheada		Atwell	J	Cpl	14 LD	Espeja
	Bently	J	Pte	14 LD	Almeida		Beard	J	Pte	14 LD	Sobral
	Bidgood	J	Pte	14 LD	POW Talavera		Bird	G	Pte	14 LD	Sabugal
							Boorch	J	Pte	14 LD	Espeja
	Billings	W	Pte	14 LD	Sexmiro		Bubb	J	Pte	14 LD	Carpio
	Blackford	J	Pte	14 LD	Almeida		Buchalong	G	Pte	14 LD	Espeja
	Blocksidge	W	Pte	14 LD	Santarem		Bunyon	W	Pte	14 LD	Carpio
	Boulken	J	Sgt	14 LD	Santarem		Cannor	J	Pte	14 LD	Oporto
	Briggs	J	Pte	14 LD	Santarem		Carter	W	Pte	14 LD	Sobral
	Brown	J	Pte	14 LD	Almeida		Compton	J	Pte	14 LD	Sobral
	Brown	W	Pte	14 LD	Sexmiro		Crawley	C	Pte	14 LD	Oporto
	Burke	F	Pte	14 LD	Sobral		Crockett	J	Pte	14 LD	Oporto
	Carleton	E	Sgt	14 LD	Sobral		Denham	J	Pte	14 LD	Oporto
	Charlton	J	Pte	14 LD	Santarem		Edwards	J	Pte	14 LD	Fuentes d'Onor
	Chilcott	T	Cpl	14 LD	Abrantes						
	Church	T	Pte	14 LD	Sobral		Elthorn	I	Pte	14 LD	Oporto
	Coats	J	Pte	14 LD	Sobral		Flanaghan	P	Pte	14 LD	Carpio
	Coghlan	J	Pte	14 LD	Santarem		Gordon	J	Pte	14 LD	Oporto
	Cornish	G	Pte	14 LD	Almeida		Gough	J	Pte	14 LD	Oporto

Year	Surname	Initial	Rank	Regiment	Place
1811	Harrison	J	Cpl	14 LD	Oporto
	Heazal	J	Pte	14 LD	Oporto
	Hinton	R	Pte	14 LD	Oporto
	Knipe	R	Capt	14 LD	Fuentes d'Onor
	Lester	J	Pte	14 LD	Oporto
	Marshall	W	Pte	14 LD	Oporto
	Nargate	H	Pte	14 LD	Oporto
	Owens	R	Pte	14 LD	Fuentes d'Onor
	Paynes	J	Pte	14 LD	Coa River
	Phillips	T	Pte	14 LD	Oporto
	Sansom	S	Pte	14 LD	Nave d'Aver
	Scales	W	Pte	14 LD	Fuentes d'Onor
	Wharton	J	Pte	14 LD	Sobral
	Winter	J	Pte	14 LD	Oporto
	Woods	E	Pte	14 LD	Oporto
1812	Ambrose	J	Pte	14 LD	Oporto
	Bailey	J	Pte	14 LD	Oporto
	Beaufoy	F	Pte	14 LD	Oporto
	Bedsworth	J	Pte	14 LD	Oporto
	Broughton-Brereton	J	Pte	14 LD	Castrillos
	Browning	T	Cpl	14 LD	Salamanca
	Burn	S	Pte	14 LD	Oporto
	Burton	J	Pte	14 LD	Oporto
	Doyle	M	Pte	14 LD	Oporto
	Duncan	W	Pte	14 LD	Oporto
	Fitzgerald	P	Pte	14 LD	Oporto
	Hawthorn	T	Pte	14 LD	Oporto
	Hill	J	Pte	14 LD	Oporto
	Lamb	T	Pte	14 LD	Oporto
	Parsons	T	Pte	14 LD	Oporto
	Ruby	J	Pte	14 LD	Oporto
	Smith	T	Pte	14 LD	Oporto
	Welling	J	Pte	14 LD	Oporto
1813	Adler	W	Pte	14 LD	Oporto
	Batchellor	C	Pte	14 LD	Oporto
	Bennett	J	Pte	14 LD	Oporto
	Bond	C	TSM	14 LD	Roncesvalles
	Card	J	Pte	14 LD	Oporto
	Farrell	P	Pte	14 LD	Oporto
	Ford	J	Pte	14 LD	Oporto
	Gibbs	A	Cpl	14 LD	Oporto
	Gibbs	J	Pte	14 LD	Oporto
	Gibson	J	Pte	14 LD	River Nive
	Gosling	J	Pte	14 LD	Oporto
	Green	J	Pte	14 LD	Oporto
	Haynes	G	Pte	14 LD	Oporto
	Jones	R	Pte	14 LD	Vittoria
	Lord	G	Pte	14 LD	Oporto
	Lovegrove	J	Pte	14 LD	Oporto
	Ludford	J	Pte	14 LD	Oporto
	Mears	J	Pte	14 LD	Vittoria
	Ockerman	C	Pte	14 LD	Vittoria
	Parrott	J	Pte	14 LD	Belem
	Possey	B	Pte	14 LD	Oporto
	Prior	J	Pte	14 LD	Oporto
	Quigley	P	Pte	14 LD	Oporto
	Rate	W	Pte	14 LD	Oporto
	Roberts	S	Pte	14 LD	Oporto
	Selbey	W	Pte	14 LD	Oporto

Year	Surname	Initial	Rank	Regiment	Place
1813	Sparks	W	Pte	14 LD	Vittoria
	Taylor	J	Pte	14 LD	Salamanca
	Thompson	J	Pte	14 LD	Burgos
	Turner	J	Pte	14 LD	Oporto
	Wilson	J	Pte	14 LD	Oporto
1814	Beckett	J	Pte	14 LD	Orthes
	Betrith	J	Pte	14 LD	Orthes
	Blair	J	Pte	14 LD	Oporto
	Boddington	W	Pte	14 LD	Pau
	Cadwalder	J	Pte	14 LD	Vittoria
	Fairchild	T	Pte	14 LD	Vittoria
	Hunt	R	Pte	14 LD	Oporto
	Lyons	W	Lt	14 LD	Vic Bigore
	May	J	Pte	14 LD	Vic Bigore
	Ryan	M	Pte	14 LD	Garris
	Smith	H	Pte	14 LD	Vic Bigore
	Smith	J	Pte	14 LD	Died in England
	Sparks	F	Pte	14 LD	Orthes
	Stephens	A	Pte	14 LD	Died as POW

SECOND SIKH WAR, 1848–1849

Year	Surname	Initial	Rank	Regiment	Place
1848	Alderton	J	Pte	14 LD	Ramnuggur
	Alpin	W	Pte	14 LD	Ramnuggur
	Bagg	R	Pte	14 LD	Ramnuggur
	Brazeur	W	Pte	14 LD	Ramnuggur
	Fitzgerald	J	Capt	14 LD	Ramnuggur
	Fox	C	Pte	14 LD	Ramnuggur
	Harwood	J	Sgt	14 LD	Ramnuggur
	Hatton	J	Pte	14 LD	Ramnuggur
	Havelock KH	W	LtCol	14 LD	Ramnuggur
	Hungerford	R	Pte	14 LD	Ramnuggur
	Jennings	B	Pte	14 LD	Ramnuggur
	Raines	J	Pte	14 LD	Ramnuggur
	Todd	W	Cpl	14 LD	Ramnuggur
	Tuttell	C	Pte	14 LD	Ramnuggur
	Ward	J	Pte	14 LD	Ramnuggur
	Williams	G	Pte	14 LD	Ramnuggur
1849	Atkins	G	Pte	14 LD	Chillian-wallah
	Cureton	A	Lt	14 LD	Chillian-wallah
	Evans	D	Pte	14 LD	Chillian-wallah
	Tookey	G	Pte	14 LD	Chillian-wallah
	Lloyd	A	Lt	14 LD	Goojerat
1850	King CB	J	LtCol	14 LD	Lahore
	Rogers	H	Pte	14 LD	Lahore

INDIAN MUTINY, 1857–1858

Year	Surname	Initial	Rank	Regiment	Place
1857	Redmayne	L	Lt	14 LD	Mundisore
1858	Barker	R	Pte	14 LD	Betwa
	Crook	W	Pte	14 LD	Koonch
	Crosby	W	Cpl	14 LD	Betwa
	Lawrence	G	Pte	14 LD	Koonch
	Leigh	J	Pte	14 LD	Betwa
	Maytum	F	Pte	14 LD	Koonch
	Ransom	T	Pte	14 LD	Betwa

Year	Surname	Initial	Rank	Regiment	Place
1858	Roxby	W	L/Sgt	14 LD	Betwa
	Topley	F	Pte	14 LD	Koonch
	Townsend	D	Pte	14 LD	Koonch
	Traylen	G	Pte	14 LD	Rathgur
	Watkin	W	Pte	14 LD	Koonch

EGYPT, SUDAN, 1885–1889

Year	Surname	Initial	Rank	Regiment	Place
1885	Akehurst	T	Pte	20 H	Suakin
	Bowron	T	Pte	20 H	Suakin
	Carey	J	TSM	20 H	Nile
	Coughlan	J	Pte	20 H	Korti
	Gower	A	Pte	20 H	Hasheen
1886	Blandford	W	Pte	20 H	Assuan
	Boynton	J	Pte	20 H	UK
	Brownlow	H	Pte	20 H	Egypt
	Bryan	C	Pte	20 H	Egypt
	Chaplin	J	Lt	20 H	Egypt
	Goddard	J	Pte	20 H	Assuan
	Hill	R	Cpl	20 H	Tofrek
	Hubbard	A	Cpl	20 H	Egypt
	Manifold	G	Pte	20 H	Egypt
	Neave	E	Sgt	20 H	Egypt
	Sharp	R	Pte	20 H	Egypt
1887	Atkins	G	Pte	20 H	Egypt
	Friend	C	L/Cpl	20 H	Egypt
	Groves	G	Pte	20 H	Egypt
	Hardy	H	Pte	20 H	Egypt
	Kite	S	S/Sgt	20 H	Egypt
	Mayes	W	Pte	20 H	Egypt
	Mulhall	H	Pte	20 H	Egypt
	Sladdin	J	Pte	20 H	Egypt
	Tudor	V	Pte	20 H	Egypt
	Wallsby	H	Pte	20 H	Egypt
	Webster	G	Cpl	20 H	Egypt
1888	Howes	F	Pte	20 H	Gemaizah
	Jordan	F	Pte	20 H	Gemaizah
	Kealey	F	Pte	20 H	Gemaizah
	Newton	E	Pte	20 H	Gemaizah
	Thomas	C	Pte	20 H	Gemaizah
1889	Bailey	R	Pte	20 H	Egypt
	Smart	R	Pte	20 H	Egypt
	Turner	H	Pte	20 H	Egypt
	Washbrooke	J	Pte	20 H	Toski
	West	E	Pte	20 H	Egypt

BOER WAR, 1899–1902

Year	Surname	Initial	Rank	Regiment	Place
1900	Amor	J	Pte	14 H	Roode Kop
	Aplin	A	Pte	14 H	Natal
	Batson	C	Cpl	14 H	Wynburg
	Bottomly		Sgt	14 H	Kameel Drift
	Bradley	J	Pte	14 H	Rhenoster Hoek
	Burton		Cpl	14 H	Kameel Drift
	Churcher	G	Pte	14 H	Naauwpoort
	Clarke	W	Pte	14 H	Pretoria
	Coe	A	Pte	14 H	Natal
	Cunningham	L	Sgt	14 H	Leeuw Kop
	Day	E	Pte	14 H	Middleburg

Year	Surname	Initial	Rank	Regiment	Place
1900	Dobson	E	Pte	14 H	Rhenoster Hoek
	Ford	A	Pte	14 H	Grootlaagte
	Ford	H	Pte	14 H	Natal
	Fort	A	Pte	14 H	Pretoria
	Goringe	S	Pte	14 H	Pretoria
	Gough the Hon, CB	G	Col	14 H	Norvals Pont
	Hadfield	H	Pte	14 H	Rietfontein
	Haken	W	Cpl	14 H	Bloem-fontein
	Hawker	F	Pte	14 H	East London
	Hemens	E	Pte	14 H	Johannes-burg
	Hyde	F	S/Sgt	14 H	Natal
	Johnson	J	Pte	14 H	Natal
	Johnson	P	Pte	14 H	Kroonstad
	Keegan	B	Pte	14 H	Geluk
	Kenworthy	V	Pte	14 H	Donkerhoek
	Lambell	W	Pte	14 H	Pretoria
	Legge CB DSO	N	LtCol	20 H	Nooitge-dacht
	Mann	W	Pte	14 H	Derdepoort
	Mears	W	Pte	14 H	Geluk
	Moore	D	Pte	14 H	Bloem-fontein
	Nutting	H	Pte	14 H	Klip Rivers-burg
	Osborne	S	Pte	14 H	Sannas Post
	Pesgood	R	Pte	14 H	Natal
	Pragnell	W	Pte	14 H	Roode Kop
	Redhead	T	Pte	14 H	Rhenoster Hoek
	Robertson	S	Capt	14 H	Kroonstad
	Seward	V	pte	14 H	Sterkstroom
	Storer	A	Sgt	14 H	Natal
	Swaine	V	Pte	14 H	Natal
	Underhill	W	Pte	14 H	East London
	Watson	J	Pte	14 H	Natal
	Wiltshire	H	Capt	20 H	Kaffir Kop
	Wood	W	Pte	14 H	Natal
1901	Beavington	J	Pte	14 H	Cape Town
	Bough	F	Pte	14 H	Witkopjes
	Butler	E	Pte	14 H	Newcastle
	Cox	H	Pte	14 H	Wynburg
	Davies	H	SQMS	14 H	Elands-fontaine
	Dunlearie	S	Pte	14 H	Mullers Pass
	Evans	J	L/Cpl	14 H	Elands-fontein
	Eves	F	Pte	14 H	Donkeys Pass
	Freeman	J	Pte	14 H	Elands-fontein
	Hill	H	Pte	14 H	Newcastle
	Holland	A	L/Cpl	14 H	Albertina
	Lace	F	Lt	14 H	Newcastle
	McAdam	W	Pte	14 H	Upper Tugela
	Mathews	J	Pte	14 H	Naaupoort
	Mathews	W	L/Cpl	14 H	Pongola
	Mauser	H	Pte	14 H	Donkeys Pass

Year	Surname	Initial	Rank	Regiment	Place
1901	Passant	W	L/Cpl	14 H	Cypherfontein
	Pavitt	J	Pte	14 H	Elandsfontein
	Robertson the Hon	H	2/Lt	14 H	Johannesburg
	Spry	W	Pte	14 H	Johannesburg
	Swan	W	Pte	14 H	Cyphersfontein
	Westlake	G	Pte	14 H	Ventersdoorp
	Williams	F	Pte	14 H	Ladysmith
1902	Brooman	B	Pte	20 H	Newcastle
	Brown	C	Far/Sgt	20 H	Bushmans River
	Cooper	J	Pte	20 H	Newcastle
	Crowther	J	Pte	14 H	Newcastle
	Hayes	A	Pte	20 H	Wilge River
	Holdforth	W	Pte	14 H	Harrismith
	Mahon	P	Pte	20 H	Newcastle
	Martin	T	Pte	20 H	Roberts Drift
	Murdoch	J	Pte	14 H	Harrismith
	Searle	W	Pte	20 H	Konigsburg
	Snowden	M	RSM	20 H	Charlestown

FIRST WORLD WAR, 1914–1919

Year	Surname	Initial	Rank	Regiment	Place
1914	Alderson	E	L/Sgt	20 H	France
	Allison	G	Pte	20 H	France
	Ansell	A	Pte	20 H	France
	Arrowsmith	P	Pte	20 H	France
	Atherton	S	Pte	20 H	France
	Bailey	S	Pte	20 H	France
	Barlow	T	Pte	20 H	France
	Bassingthwaite	G	Sgt	20 H	France
	Brookes	l	Pte	14 H	France
	Brooks	M	Pte	20 H	France
	Broom	W	Pte	14 H	France
	Carew	F	2/lt	20 H	France
	Carton	D	Pte	20 H	France
	Cawley	J	Maj	20 H	France
	Charlotte	P	Sad/Cpl	20 H	France
	Christy DSO	S	Capt	20 H	France
	Cowan	R	Pte	20 H	France
	Dawson	W	Pte	20 H	France
	Fenner	W	Pte	20 H	France
	Fenton	C	Pte	20 H	France
	Fergusson	T	L/Cpl	20 H	France
	Foster	G	Pte	20 H	France
	Foster	J	Pte	20 H	France
	Garness	W	L/Cpl	20 H	France
	Garty	S	Pte	20 H	France
	Graham	J	Pte	20 H	France
	Grainger	R	Pte	20 H	France
	Grove	S	Pte	20 H	France
	Hall	J	Pte	20 H	France
	Hallet	H	Pte	20 H	France
	Hather	F	L/Cpl	20 H	France
	Hawkesworth	W	Pte	20 H	France
	Higgleton	H	Pte	20 H	France
	Jones	E	Pte	20 H	France
1914	Keen	W	Pte	20 H	France
	Lamb	R	Pte	20 H	France
	Lambert	J	Pte	20 H	France
	Lawrence	E	Pte	20 H	France
	Mansfield	H	Pte	20 H	France
	Mason	R	Pte	20 H	France
	McFall	J	Pte	20 H	France
	McLeod	W	Pte	20 H	France
	McVay	T	Pte	20 H	France
	Mercer	H	Pte	20 H	France
	Modd	G	Pte	20 H	France
	Monaghan	H	Pte	20 H	France
	Owens	W	L/Cpl	14 H	France
	Parlour	A	Pte	20 H	France
	Patterson	A	Pte	14 H	France
	Pearson	J	Pte	20 H	France
	Perman	F	L/Cpl	20 H	France
	Pickavance	P	Pte	14 H	France
	Piggot	H	L/Cpl	14 H	France
	Rayson	F	L/Cpl	20 H	France
	Reed	T	Pte	20 H	France
	Rouse	A	Pte	20 H	France
	Rose	S	L/Cpl	20 H	France
	Ryan	C	Pte	20 H	France
	Smith	F	Pte	20 H	France
	Soames	H	Lt	20 H	France
	Stevenson	J	Pte	14 H	France
	Struit	H	Pte	20 H	France
	Taunt	A	Pte	14 H	France
	Todd	A	Pte	20 H	France
	Tyrell	E	Pte	14 H	France
	Williams	F	Pte	20 H	France
	Woodbine	R	pte	20 H	France
	Yates	H	L/Cpl	20 H	France
1915	Allen	A	Pte	14 H	Mespot
	Arnott	G	SSM	20 H	UK
	Arrigoni	A	Pte	20 H	France
	Atherton	C	Pte	20 H	France
	Austin	G	Pte	20 H	France
	Barnes	J	Pte	20 H	France
	Blackburn	B	Pte	20 H	France
	Boocock	G	Pte	14 H	Mespot
	Brown	J	Pte	14 H	France
	Bruford	J	L/Cpl	20 H	France
	Bunce	F	Pte	20 H	France
	Campbell DSO	W	Maj	14 H	France
	Catley	F	Pte	20 H	France
	Clarke	A	Pte	20 H	France
	Dickenson	J	Pte	14 H	Mespot
	Dutton	H	Sad/Cpl	14 H	India
	Dutton	T	Pte	20 H	France
	Edwards	A	Pte	14 H	France
	Egerton	F	Pte	14 H	Mespot
	Evans	A	L/Cpl	20 H	France
	Everard	T	L/Cpl	20 H	France
	Gibbon	J	L/Cpl	20 H	France
	Goode	L	Pte	20 H	France
	Guest	R	Pte	14 H	UK
	Hadley	T	Cpl	20 H	France
	Hart	B	Pte	20 H	France
	Jackson	J	Pte	20 H	France
	Joys	A	Pte	20 H	France
	Kenworthy	C	Pte	20 H	France

Year	Surname	Initial	Rank	Regiment	Place	Year	Surname	Initial	Rank	Regiment	Place
1915	Lill	J	Pte	20 H	France	1916	Martin	H	Pte	20 H	France
	Mack	A	Cpl	14 H	Mespot		McFarlane	H	Pte	14 H	Mespot
	McColgan	C	Pte	14 H	France		McGrath	T	L/Sgt	14 H	Mespot
	Miles	E	Pte	20 H	France		Mewburn	S	Capt	14 H	Mespot
	Miller	J	Pte	14 H	Mespot		Mitchell	G	Cpl	14 H	Mespot
	Milner	C	Pte	20 H	France		Nottage	W	Pte	20 H	France
	Morris	G	Pte	20 H	France		Pittuck	W	Pte	20 H	France
	Mutter	L	Cpl	20 H	France		Powell	N	Pte	14 H	Mespot
	Overton	J	Pte	14 H	Mespot		Power	R	Pte	20 H	France
	Patterson	A	Pte	14 H	France		Proven	S	Pte	14 H	Mespot
	Peirson	A	L/Cpl	14 H	France		Read	L	Pte	20 H	France
	Robertson	J	L/Cpl	14 H	Mespot		Reader	J	Pte	20 H	France
	Rock	W	Pte	20 H	France		Roberts	E	Pte	14 H	Mespot
	Rogers	H	L/Cpl	20 H	France		Rogers	C	Pte	14 H	Mespot
	Shaw	S	L/Cpl	14 H	France		Saker	C	L/Cpl	14 H	Mespot
	Smith	C	Pte	14 H	France		Seagrave	J	Pte	14 H	Mespot
	Stanesby	W	Cpl	20 H	France		Seddon	E	Pte	14 H	Mespot
	Sutton	M	Pte	14 H	France		Silvester	C	Pte	14 H	Mespot
	Tester	J	Sgt	20 H	France		Smith	E	Sgt	14 H	Mespot
	Wadeson	W	Pte	20 H	France		Stevenson	I	Pte	14 H	Mespot
	Walker	J	Cpl	20 H	France		Thompson	J	Cpl	14 H	Mespot
	Walton	W	Pte	20 H	France		Todd	H	Pte	14 H	Mespot
	Warner	C	Pte	20 H	France		Toon	J	Pte	14 H	Mespot
	Wilson	W	L/Cpl	14 H	India		White	S	Pte	14 H	Mespot
	Wood	P	Pte	20 H	France		Wiford	F	Pte	20 H	France
1916	Baker	S	Pte	14 H	France		Willan	E	Sadd	14 H	Mespot
	Barnes	H	Pte	20 H	France		Wilson	J	Pte	14 H	Mespot
	Bennett	H	Pte	14 H	Mespot	1917	Adams	W	L/Cpl	20 H	France
	Boland	W	Pte	20 H	France		Allston	J	Pte	20 H	France
	Bradley	C	Pte	20 H	France		Astley	A	Capt	14 H	Mespot
	Bradshaw	J	Pte	14 H	Mespot		Austen DCM	E	2/Lt	14 H	India
	Briggs	F	Pte	20 H	France		Baker	J	Sgt	14 H	Mespot
	Brooke	S	Pte	20 H	France		Barker	J	L/Cpl	20 H	France
	Brown	C	Pte	20 H	France		Barne MC	S	Capt	20 H	France
	Brown	G	L/Cpl	20 H	France		Bollington	J	Pte	14 H	Mespot
	Deakin	C	2/Lt	14 H	Mespot		Bowden	W	Pte	14 H	Mespot
	Drewitt	G	Pte	14 H	Mespot		Brown	H	Sgt	20 H	France
	Dunmore	H	Pte	20 H	France		Bruce	T	Capt	14 H	Mespot
	Eveleigh	H	L/Cpl	20 H	France		Burt	W	Pte	14 H	Mespot
	Ferris	A	Pte	20 H	France		Butters	G	Pte	20 H	France
	Flynn	J	L/Cpl	20 H	France		Byron	J	Pte	20 H	France
	Gale	H	S/Sgt	14 H	Mespot		Clarey	J	L/Cpl	20 H	France
	Graves	W	Cpl	20 H	France		Clarke	J	Pte	20 H	France
	Hadley	F	SQMS	14 H	Mespot		Etherington	D	Pte	14 H	Mespot
	Hall	F	Cpl	14 H	Mespot		Forbes	G	Pte	20 H	France
	Hatherall	E	Pte	20 H	France		Foulstone	F	Pte	14 H	Mespot
	Hayhurst	J	L/Cpl	20 H	France		Francis	J	Sgt	14 H	Mespot
	Hearing	T	Pte	20 H	France		Goodwin	A	Pte	20 H	France
	Holloway	E	Pte	14 H	India		Gudgeon	E	Pte	20 H	France
	Holmes	C	Pte	14 H	Mespot		Green	W	L/Cpl	14 H	Mespot
	James	G	Pte	14 H	UK		Hancock	J	Pte	20 H	France
	Jeffrey	G	2/Lt	20 H	France		Hardy	J	Pte	14 H	Mespot
	Johns	A	S/Sgt	14 H	Mespot		Havelock	R	Pte	20 H	France
	Jones	A	Pte	14 H	Mespot		Hewitt DSO	R	LtCol	14 H	Mespot
	Kay	D	Pte	20 H	France		Holbrook	M	Pte	20 H	France
	Keightly	A	Pte	20 H	France		Holden	E	Sad/Cpl	20 H	France
	Leigh	H	SQMS	14 H	Mespot		Holmes	A	Pte	14 H	Mespot
	Lendren	G	Pte	20 H	France		Holmes	C	Pte	20 H	France
	Locke	C	Pte	20 H	France		Houghton	A	Sgt/Tptr	14 H	Mespot
	Lowe	W	Pte	14 H	Mespot		Howarth	J	L/Cpl	14 H	Mespot
	Lucking	W	Sgt	20 H	France		Jeram	A	Pte	20 H	France
	Mallalien	J	Pte	20 H	France		Johnson	J	Pte	14 H	Mespot
	Mann	H	Pte	14 H	Mespot		Jolly	F	Pte	20 H	France

Year	Surname	Initial	Rank	Regiment	Place
1917	Keatly	C	Sgt	20 H	France
	Kirk	W	Pte	20 H	France
	Knowles	P	Pte	14 H	India
	Laggett	W	Sgt	14 H	Mespot
	Lathbury	J	Pte	20 H	France
	Lewis	R	Pte	14 H	Mespot
	Leventon	F	Pte	20 H	France
	Littlemore	I	Pte	20 H	France
	Mackay	J	Pte	14 H	Mespot
	Mantle	H	Cpl	14 H	Mespot
	Marsh	J	Pte	14 H	Mespot
	McWilliams	A	Sgt	14 H	Mespot
	Meade	R	Lt	14 H	Mespot
	North	E	Sgt	14 H	Mespot
	Osgood	S	Pte	20 H	France
	Pattison	J	Cpl	14 H	Mespot
	Plyer	A	Pte	14 H	Mespot
	Pryce	H	L/Cpl	14 H	Mespot
	Rasell	R	Pte	20 H	France
	Richards	J	Sgt	14 H	Mespot
	Rose	A	Pte	20 H	France
	Saunders	H	Sgt	20 H	France
	Senior	W	Pte	20 H	France
	Shanks	T	Pte	14 H	Mespot
	Silvertop MC	W	Capt	20 H	France
	Slater	W	Pte	14 H	Mespot
	Stanley	R	Pte	14 H	Mespot
	Sykes	G	Pte	20 H	France
	Thornton	R	Sgt	14 H	Mespot
	Walker	J	Pte	14 H	France
	Watsham	H	Pte	20 H	France
	Wilkins	W	Pte	14 H	Mespot
	Willocks	G	Pte	14 H	France
	Wilson-Gill	T	Sgt	14 H	Mespot
	Woolf	C	2/Lt	20 H	France
	Wright	G	Pte	14 H	Mespot
	Wright	P	Pte	14 H	Mespot
1918	Allsop	W	Pte	20 H	France
	Andrews	W	Pte	20 H	France
	Ball	H	Pte	20 H	France
	Batten	E	Pte	20 H	France
	Billinghurst	H	Pte	20 H	France
	Bion	R	Lt	20 H	France
	Blackburn	A	Pte	20 H	France
	Carpenter	A	Pte	20 H	France
	Carr	A	Pte	14 H	Mespot
	Cheesman	W	Pte	20 H	France
	Clancy	E	Tptr	20 H	France
	Cole	A	Cpl	14 H	India
	Collins	M	Pte	14 H	India
	Cook CMG DSO	G	Lt/Col	20 H	France
	Corney	E	L/Cpl	20 H	France
	Cox	A	Pte	20 H	France
	Cox	G	L/Cpl	20 H	France
	Crellin	J	Pte	20 H	France
	Cross	A	Pte	20 H	France
	Curzon	T	Pte	20 H	France
	Daines	H	L/Cpl	20 H	France
	Davies	T	Pte	14 H	Mespot
	Devey	J	Pte	14 H	India
	Eyles	W	S/Sgt	14 H	Mespot
	Ferneley	E	Pte	20 H	France
	Fish	S	Pte	20 H	France
1918	Fisher	C	Pte	14 H	Mespot
	Foulkes	F	Pte	20 H	France
	Gissing	A	Pte	20 H	France
	Grant	W	Pte	20 H	France
	Griffiths	J	Pte	14 H	India
	Hall	E	Pte	14 H	Mespot
	Harrison	J	Pte	14 H	India
	Hill	M	Pte	20 H	France
	Hoff	B	Cpl	14 H	India
	Holt	A	Pte	14 H	Mespot
	Jackson	D	Lt	20 H	France
	Jobson	G	Pte	14 H	Mespot
	Jones	E	Pte	20 H	France
	Jordan	C	L/Cpl	20 H	France
	Kelly	L	Pte	20 H	France
	Kirk	R	Pte	20 H	France
	Lees	J	Pte	14 H	India
	LeGry	H	Pte	14 H	Mespot
	Logan	T	Pte	20 H	France
	Longthorne	J	Pte	14 H	Mespot
	Lupton	A	Pte	14 H	Mespot
	Lyte	G	Pte	14 H	Mespot
	Mathews	A	Pte	20 H	France
	Maughan	E	Pte	20 H	France
	Mann	C	Lt	20 H	France
	May	A	Cpl	20 H	France
	Mcintosh	K	Pte	14 H	Mespot
	Moss	H	Sgt	20 H	France
	Mullen	J	Cpl	14 H	Mespot
	Nickson	C	Pte	20 H	France
	Ogilvy	W	Lt	20 H	France
	Ormsby	W	Pte	20 H	France
	Pearson	W	Cpl	14 H	Mespot
	Ralli	L	Lt	20 H	France
	Riley	S	Pte	14 H	Mespot
	Ringham	C	L/Cpl	20 H	France
	Sadler	C	Pte	20 H	France
	Simmons	J	Pte	14 H	Mespot
	Slaughter	G	Pte	14 H	Mespot
	Smith	W	Pte	20 H	France
	Sodern	W	Pte	20 H	France
	Stanford	W	Cpl	20 H	France
	Steeples	S	Pte	14 H	Mespot
	Stockdale	S	Pte	20 H	France
	Sturgess	J	Pte	20 H	France
	Tasker	J	Cpl	20 H	France
	Taylor	W	Pte	20 H	France
	Thompson	J	Pte	14 H	Mespot
	Thompson	R	S/Sgt	20 H	France
	Thompson	W	Pte	20 H	France
	Thornton	G	Pte	14 H	Mespot
	Wagstaffe	J	Pte	14 H	India
	Walley	C	Pte	20 H	France
	Watkins	F	Pte	20 H	France
	Webb	A	Cpl	20 H	France
	Williams	D	L/Cpl	14 H	Mespot
	Wombwell	A	L/Cpl	20 H	France
1919	Ashton	J	Pte	14 H	Mespot
	Eales	J	L/Cpl	14 H	Mespot

Year	Surname	Initial	Rank	Regiment	Place
SECOND WORLD WAR, 1939–1945					
1939	Richardson	A	L/Cpl	14/20 H	India
1941	Armitage	J	Tpr	14/20 H	Persia
	Doran	J	Sgt	14/20 H	Persia
	Gilyeat	G	Tpr	14/20 H	Middle East
	Haddon	A	Cpl	14/20 H	Persia
	Hiddingh	A	Maj	14/20 H	Middle East
	McAllen	R	Capt	14/20 H	Iraq
	McDowell	W	Cpl	14/20 H	Persia
	Parry-Crooke	J	Capt	14/20 H	Persia
	Timms	C	Tpr	14/20 H	India
1942	Glen-Murphy	J	Tpr	14/20 H	Iraq
	Lockwood	J	Tpr	14/20 H	Iraq
	Salway	T	Tpr	14/20 H	Iraq
1943	Cooper	E	Tpr	14/20 H	Middle East
	Stevens	A	Tpr	14/20 H	Middle East
1944	Ascott	D	Tpr	14/20 H	Middle East
	Champion	R	Tpr	14/20 H	Middle East
	Lloyd	R	Tpr	14/20 H	Middle East
	Silvertop DSO MC	D	Lt/Col	14/20 H	Holland

Year	Surname	Initial	Rank	Regiment	Place
1944	Stanton	A	Capt	14/20 H	New Guinea
1945	Annal	F	Sgt	14/20 H	Italy
	Banks	V	Tpr	14/20 H	Italy
	Burt	J	Tpr	14/20 H	Italy
	Eston	R	Sgt	14/20 H	Italy
	Hampson	A	Tpr	14/20 H	Italy
	Long	A	SSM	14/20 H	Italy
	Murray	J	Tpr	14/20 H	Italy
	Nixon	C	Tpr	14/20 H	Italy
	Shepstone	W	Cpl	14/20 H	Italy
	Smith	H	Tpr	14/20 H	Italy

NORTHERN IRELAND, 1970–1992

Year	Surname	Initial	Rank	Regiment	Place
1971	Armstrong	I	Cpl	14/20 H	N Ireland
	Platt	J	Sgt	14/20 H	N Ireland
1972	Williams-Wynn	R	2/Lt	14/20 H	N Ireland
1974	Cotton	M	Cpl	14/20 H	N Ireland
	Herbert	M	Cpl	14/20 H	N Ireland
	Tyson	J	Tpr	14/20 H	N Ireland

Above: The Regimental Chapel in Barton Church (Norwyn Photographics)

BIBLIOGRAPHY

Anglesea, Seventh Marquess of. *A History of the British Cavalry 1816–1919*, London, Leo Cooper, 1973

Cannon, Richard. *Historical Record of the 14th, or King's, Regiment of Light Dragoons*

Compton, Herbert. *A King's Hussar*

Daniell, Christopher. *A Traveller's History of England*

Darling, Major J. C. *20th Hussars in the Great War*

— *A Short History of the 14th/20th King's Hussars, 1715–1950*

Fraser, Antonia (ed.) *The Kings and Queens of England*

Hamilton, Colonel H. B. *Historical Record of the 14th (King's) Hussars 1715–1900*

Harris, John. *The Indian Mutiny*

Hill, Douglas John. *Nobody's Own*

Longford, Lady Elizabeth. *Wellington: The Years of the Sword*, London, 1971

Miller, Major J. A. T. (ed.) *Historical Record of the 14th (King's) Hussars 1900–1922*

Nolan, Dr Edward H. *History of the British Empire in India and the East*

Oatts, Lieutenant-Colonel L. B. *The Emperor's Chambermaids*

Perrett, Bryan. *The Hawks*

Pimlott, John. *The Guinness History of the British Army*

The Hawk Journals of the *14th/20th King's Hussars*, 1948–1991

The King's Royal Hussars Journal, 1993

INDEX